A Camera in the Dales

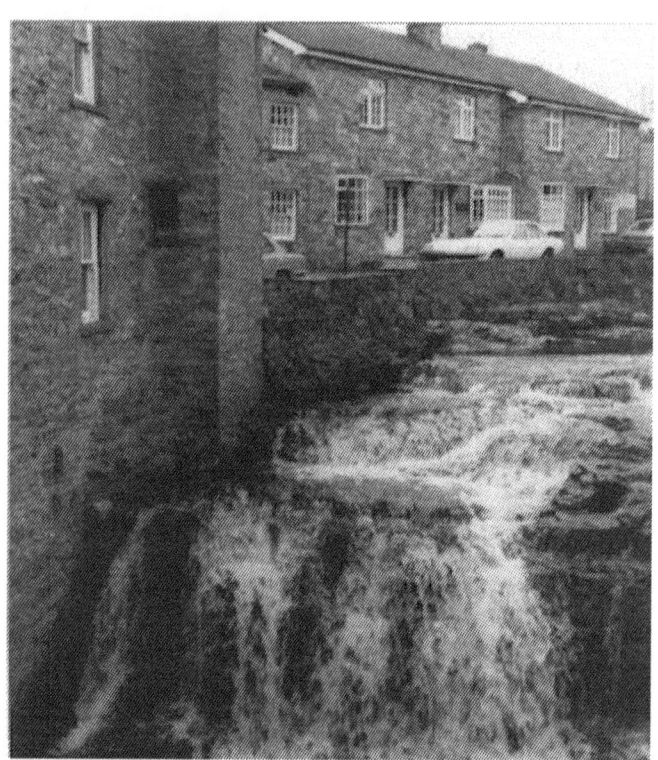

Waterfall in Hawes. The building that is a
shop is built straight out of the beck bottom.

A Camera in the Dales

A Photographic Record

John Moore

Editor:
Charles Muller, MA (Wales), PhD (Lond),
DLitt (OFS), DEd (SA)

Writers Club Press
San Jose New York Lincoln Shanghai

A Camera in the Dales
A Photographic Record

Published by Writers Club Press
an imprint of iUniverse.com, Inc.

For information address:
iUniverse.com, Inc.
620 North 48th Street
Suite 201
Lincoln, NE 68504-3467
www.iuniverse.com

Photographs are by John Moore.

ISBN: 0-595-12892-0

Printed in the United States of America

Dedication

*To Myra, a frequent companion during my photographic excursions,
and without whom this book would not have been possible.*

Epigraph

Beauty is God's handwriting
(Seen on a wayside pulpit.)

Foreword

> "It was by mere chance that I took up photography. The anti-smoking campaign was not heard of then, but as smoking appeared to be troubling my stomach I was thinking of giving it up. I discussed it with my wife Myra and she said, "Put away the money every day which you save." So I did. I stopped smoking and put the money away every day. Although cigarettes in the 'fifties were much cheaper than today, it wasn't very long before I had £20 in my little box."
>
> John Moore

When he gave up smoking John Moore was able to buy a camera with the money he saved. This book, with its 56 monochrome photographs of the Yorkshire dales and dales life, is the result! The book is more than a colourful survey of the dales—it is a potted history, for many anecdotes, picaresque characters and old customs are captured here—through the lens of the camera and the sensitive mind of the author. The reader will be taken back not only to the days of Lady Anne Clifford, to the days of the carthorse and the blacksmith, but will witness the passing of the steam railway and the changing seasons in what must be one of the most beautiful parts of England.

Charles Muller

1

The meadows were a blaze of buttercups when I had my first glimpse of the dales. It was one of those narrow dales where the fields rise steeply from the road and where whitewashed farmhouses tuck snugly into the hillside. For years I had lived within fifty miles of the dales, yet I had never seen this unique countryside.

A few years later my wife and I bought a small business in a small dales town...Hawes, at the head of Wensleydale. Here we saw the dales in their many moods as we lived and worked among the dales folk for over twenty years.

Duerley beck runs through Hawes. It drops over a small waterfall right against a shop built out of the beck bottom. This is where we lived when we first came to Hawes. Most of the time the fall sounded like a kettle boiling gently, but when there was a flood it roared; and when the rocks started rumbling over the solid limestone bottom it was more like thunder!

A little upstream from the waterfall the beck once turned a mill wheel. The outside of the building is very much as it was but the inside has been converted into modern flats. In summer, visitors often line the bridge a few yards downstream, watching the fish in the lucid pool below the fall. On the other side of this bridge there used to be another mill; since no building or space is ever wasted in Hawes, this is now the Conservative club. I found an old photo of this mill wheel taken more than seventy years ago: though the wheel has gone, very little has changed.

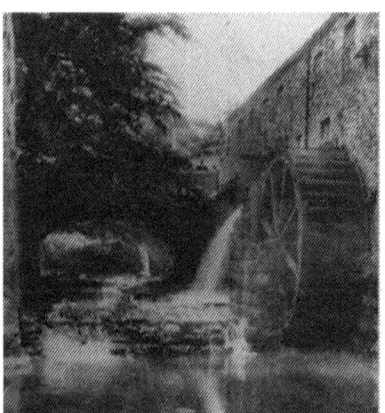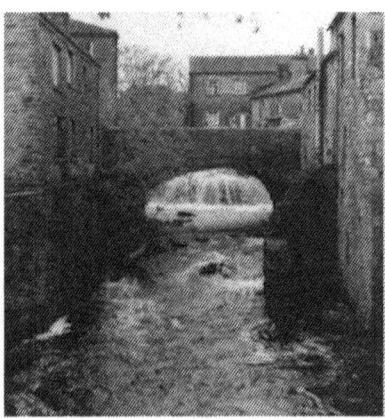

Water Wheel in Hawes at the turn of the century—and as it is today.

Half a mile upstream from the waterfall is the tiny village of Gayle. Although so close to Hawes, it has always clung tenaciously to its own identity. It's a closely-knit community whose inhabitants regard Hawes just down the road as virtually another country. I remember an old lady who moved to Hawes from Gayle; when I asked her if she had settled in her new home, she replied, "Oh no, the folk aren't like the Gayle folk"— as if Hawes were a hundred miles away! There was a time when they had their own football team and billiards team; also, any Hawes boy who was so bold as to come courting a Gayle girl was promptly chased out of the village!

The bridge is the focal point of the village. If the weather is reasonable there will always be two or three villagers chatting there. There's the story of a stranger who once asked a man on the bridge if he could tell him where Richard Iveson lived. Now there are an awful lot of Ivesons in Gayle—known mostly by their nicknames, a not unreasonable state of affairs, really, with so many people of the same surname. Well, the Gayle man went through all the Ivesons in his mind and confessed that he couldn't place this particular one. As the stranger turned to go, however, he exclaimed, "Wait a minute, that's *me!*"

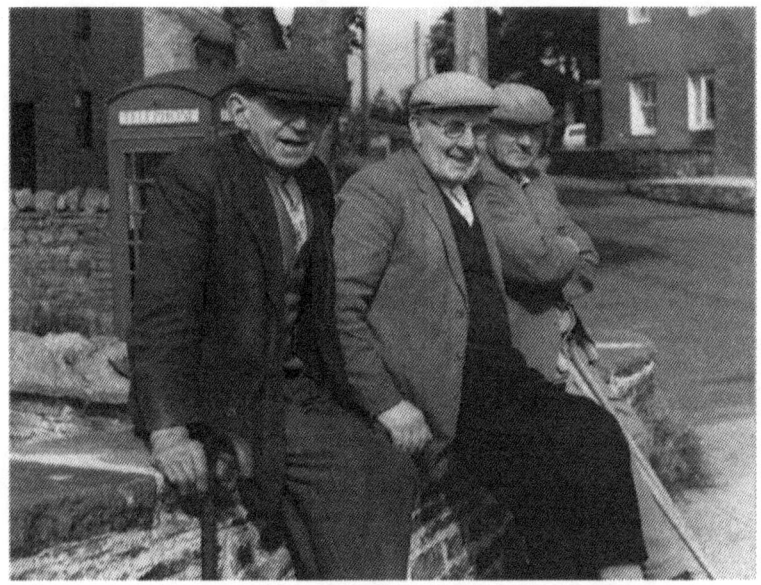

Gayle Bridge is a great meeting place for the village.

I like the people of Gayle. They're sturdy individualists but always friendly and hospitable. One is an old friend of ours, always known as

Annie Mary whom I photographed beside her old iron range which today is a collector's piece. I was never in her house long before I was given a cup of tea and a piece of 'Gayle bannock,' the pastry so well liked by the folk there. She worked for us at the market for many years until her husband was taken ill, when she devoted the rest of her life to looking after him.

Most artists' impressions of Gayle are from this bridge, as one can see in nearly any exhibition of dales art. I took photos there, all round Gayle too, but most of all I was attracted to the geese which I could never resist, either on their own or to make an attractive foreground to any picture. They are a feature of the village. Indeed, Gayle is famous for its geese. In the past many were kept there and no doubt were a welcome addition to the villagers' income.

I've been told that in times past when so many of the villagers kept geese, there would be a hole in the pantry wall: when a goose came to sit she could have a nest under the stone pantry shelves, and could come and go as she pleased—to eat and to drink—through this purpose-built doorway. In season there would be a sizeable flock and they would be driven out to pasture and brought home in the evening, just like cattle. At the time I took my photos I think only Annie Mary still kept geese so that these would be hers which stayed in the beck and round the village all day.

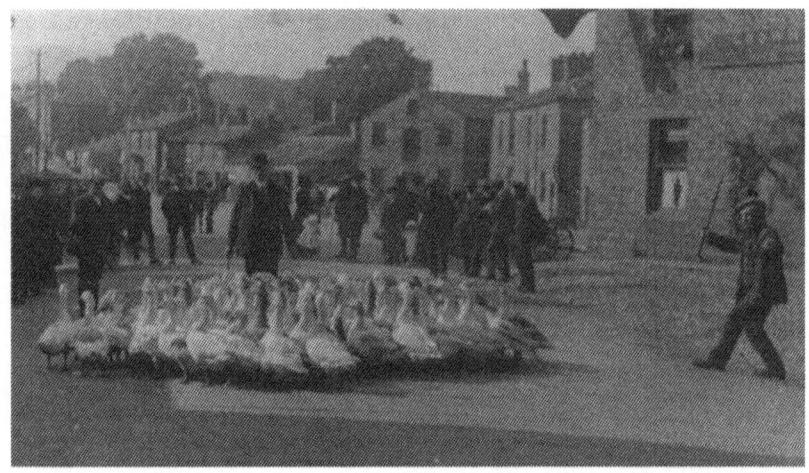

Geese gathered together in Hawes market place before their journey down the dale.
From an old photograph.

Before World War I, when the harvest was gathered in, geese were driven to Hawes and sold to the lower country down the dale. A local historian told me that the buyer, having assembled his flock, would have them walk through tar and then sand so that they were shod for their journey; they would then be driven to the corn-growing farms, to be fattened on stubble and sold piecemeal until the whole flock had been disposed of.

Between Gayle and Hawes there is yet another mill—but here the waterwheel was replaced at the turn of the century with a water turbine. The owners must have been go-ahead people, for they started to generate electricity for the immediate district—a great innovation in such a community and at that time. The electricity was used mostly for lighting and the plant was shut down every night at midnight, unless there was a dance or some special function that merited an extension of time.

Before the First World War Hawes had a gas supply, now long forgotten, the only trace being the odd glimpse of an old gas pipe. Unfortunately the gas was generated by carbide, for when all available carbide was required by the war effort, the company had to close down. Meanwhile the enterprising electric company had installed electricity into many of the houses and had even put lights on poles throughout the town—so electricity took over and the gasworks never started again.

Incidentally, the old turbine is still in use, driving machinery for a small joinery business. When in 1977 the owners overhauled the turbine it was found that only one part needed replacing. The makers of the turbine were found to be still in business in Kendal and they readily supplied and re-installed the part. As far as I know the turbine is still doing its job as well as ever.

2

When we came to Hawes in the 'fifties it was a self-contained little town. The population was only about 1000—but if you were to suggest it was a village you were soon told it was a *town*, as indeed it is. It was granted a market charter in 1684. I've seen the document and photographed it together with its magnificent seal. There were joiners, builders, a shoemaker, a blacksmith, a rope maker, a tailor, a small cheese factory and, of course, cafes, pubs and a variety of shops. They all relied on one another, the local inhabitants and the farming community for bread and butter, whereas the jam, you might say, came from the tourists!

Before the days of cars the railway put Hawes on the map for the tourist trade, connecting it with Northallerton in the East and the famous Carlisle-Settle railway in the West. Even before the First World War the district had its own guidebook, packed with adverts of guest-houses, B & B's and local shops. There were few cars about in those days and rationing had only just finished. Nevertheless, austerity was beginning to lift. Holiday crowds came by bus on day trips and these, with walkers and cyclists, brought a welcome influx of money. Nowadays the dales are so popular, with so many owning cars and holiday cottages that the season has been extended, giving an enormous boost to the economy of the dales.

Our arrival in the 'fifties was before this enhanced popularity. The business we had taken over consisted of a small general shop and a cafe where, like all the others in town, we used to welcome the arrival of Easter with its flood of visitors.

It was by mere chance that I took up photography. The anti-smoking campaign was not heard of then, but as smoking appeared to be troubling my stomach I was thinking of giving it up. I discussed it with my wife and she said, "Put away the money every day which you save." So I did. I stopped smoking and put the money away every day. Although cigarettes in the 'fifties were much cheaper than today, it wasn't very long before I had £20 in my little box.

I've always been interested in photography. As a boy I saved up 10/6 and bought a box Brownie. Now, with over £20 in my pocket, I launched out and bought a Vito B 35mm camera. After running a film through and seeing the results, I was well and truly hooked: I read every photographic book on which I could lay my hands, picked the brains of any fellow photographer, joined a camera club and looked at the world through the lens of a camera. Soon all my friends and neighbours became accustomed to seeing me in unusual positions taking what surely looked like unlikely photographs.

Very nervously I started to develop my own films. I bought an enlarger and the possibilities now seemed endless as a whole new world opened out before me. Then, one evening when I was out for one of my walks that were really expeditions in search of fresh photos, I met the local Brownie pack of which one of my daughters was a keen member. They were taking a break from their activities and, seeing my camera, Brown Owl laughingly suggested that I photograph the group. I presented her with a copy and I was delighted when she ordered one for each member of the group—*and* insisted I be paid for the photos! At the time I didn't see this as a serious commercial proposition, but when I began to receive orders for children's photos and odd photographic jobs, I began to wonder of there was something in this photography business.

Even in a small place a surprising number of events take place in the course of a year. There was and still is an operatic society which presents a musical in Hawes every year. Once there was an annual pantomime; also, a drama club which staged regular performances. All these showed a variety of local talent.

These events took place in the market hall. What a useful place that was and still is! As well as providing a stage for these various productions, it is the venue for stalls on market day. Some evenings it is a badminton court. Wedding receptions are sometimes held there, too, and in the days before TV it was the local cinema for two shows a week. Prices were then 7p. for ordinary seats and 8p. on the stage, the screen being at the other end of the hall over the door.

Sometimes a picture of these productions would appear in the local paper, but many small items or anything needing a man on the spot were never photographed. I started to take some of these events and having sent them in to the paper was delighted to see them published. Soon I was taking all the press pictures in the district which, of course, was a big help in my becoming known as the local photographer.

Up to this time I had only photographed what I fancied and by the use of much midnight electricity and my wife's patience and encouragement had learnt a good deal about printing. However, I found that there is a big difference between taking a few shots of my own choice and having to produce a set of acceptable prints under what were very often difficult circumstances. Things were seldom straightforward and I had to learn to overcome the various problems that could arise.

In those early days I had much trouble with temperamental flashguns that didn't flash at the vital moment. There seemed to be so many dodgy connections, and if they were sound then the bulbs would play up. Most of my presswork was inside some building where a flashgun was indispensable. To stand up to take a group, perhaps in a hall full of people, have everything set, and then find that the flash didn't flash, was a very traumatic experience.

I discovered that presentations produced problems that I had never dreamt of. Perhaps a lady would be opening some function where I had to photograph the child presenting her with a bouquet. The lady would make her speech and, as the applause died down, the child would be urged forward with the bouquet. I would have chosen what I considered a strategic position when the little girl (it was usually a girl) would promptly maneuver herself into a position where it was impossible for me to see a thing. I became used to this and, like many other photographers, would wait until the initial presentation was over before setting things up to my own satisfaction.

I once had an assignment to take photos for identity cards for a dozen members of a voluntary organisation. We arranged to use the back room of a little pub where I arrived in good time and set up my gear. When the members arrived—all men—the leader of the group consulted his instructions and found that all photos were supposed to be taken in the official shirt—rather a problem since only one man had turned up in the necessary garment. This was no obstacle to the resourceful group, nevertheless: doing eleven quick changes, each man was photographed in the same shirt. Rather remarkable, perhaps, that the same shirt fitted twelve men—and that the photos turned out to be quite acceptable!

3

Hawes lost its railway in the early 'sixties. First the line that connected it with the Carlisle-Settle railway was taken up. Shortly afterwards the last train from the Northallerton end of the line drew into the station. The coaches were packed with railway enthusiasts who swarmed all over the station taking photos. Before long they piled back into the train, departing the way they had come, and the age of the train for Hawes was over.

Soon the remainder of the lines, the signal box and even the bridges were gone. The station with its booking office and waiting room were abandoned to decay. Where in the past there had been prize-winning flowerbeds, rosebay willow herb flourished, and in the booking hall a blackbird built its nest in the aperture once occupied by the station clock.

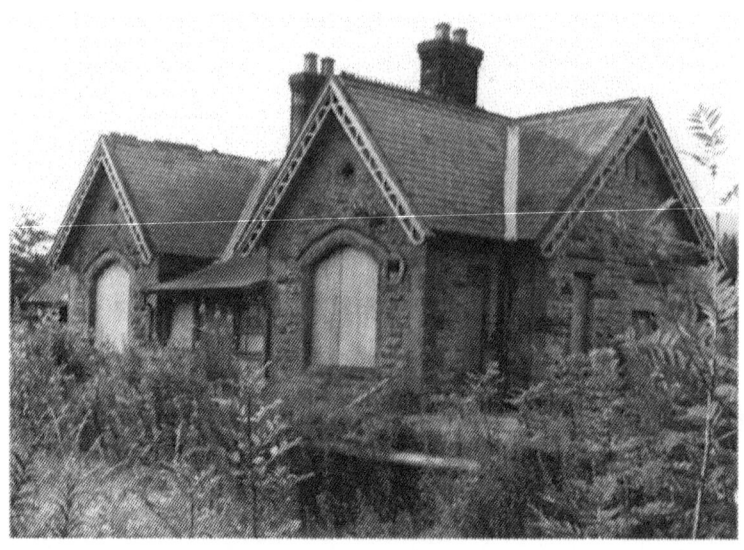

Hawes station when nature took over.

For over ten years nature had her way and those who would have loved to turn the old station into a house were turned down when they applied for permission. However, in the late seventies, the National Parks took over the station, turning the booking hall and waiting rooms into an information centre. The old warehouse that stands in the station yard was in good structural condition, so it was turned into a museum for dales artifacts.

Two well-known local historians lived in the dale—Marie Hartley and Joan Ingleby. For years they rescued many old farm and household tools from the rubbish heap. They attended farm sales, buying old farm gear for which there was no longer any use, saving many unique items whenever they had the opportunity. Eventually they had not only a comprehensive collection but an embarrassingly large one. For years they had looked for a suitable building in which to house this collection where it could be properly exhibited; so the old railway warehouse was the perfect answer—especially since the building itself was of historical interest.

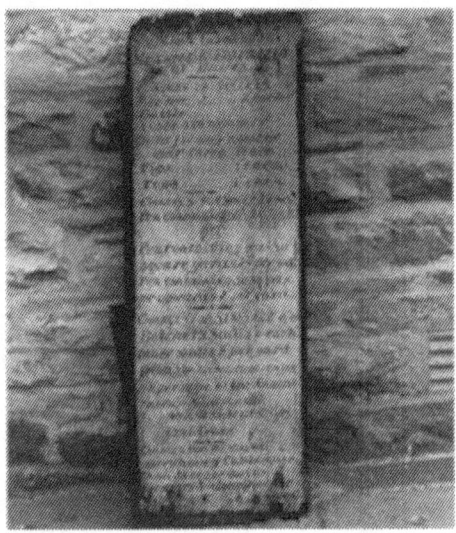

The Old Market toll board, rescued from the rubbish cart by Kit Calvert, now in Hawes museum.

4

Present everyday life becomes history in just a few years. There are many things I wish I had recorded, but at least I'm glad of those that I did—particularly local craftsmen at work. The blacksmith was one, and a blacksmith at work always makes a good picture.

There is one job our blacksmith was called upon to undertake which is only required in sheep country. That is, the making of branding irons with which a farmer burns his registered initials into the sheep's horn. Since all the sheep in the district were horned sheep that ran on the open fell, this was a very necessary practice. The blacksmith would carve out the initials on the iron, and then test it on the little door just outside his shop. In his time he must have made a great many of these irons and so the door is covered with these testings that must constitute a history in itself. Happily, this door has been preserved in the little museum at Hawes.

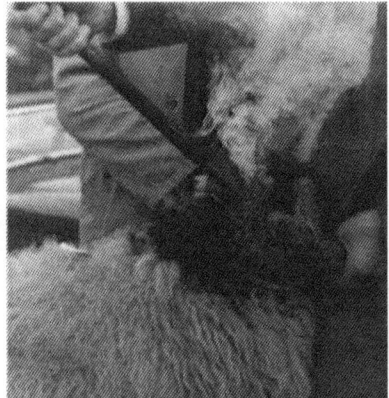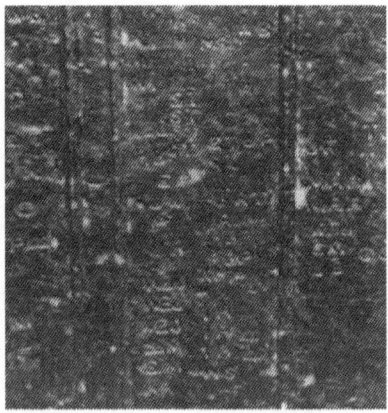

Hornburning (left); and the door on which the blacksmith tried out his hornburns.

5

The market place at Hawes was once the cattle market. Where stalls now stand on a Tuesday there were pens of sheep and there was an extremely heavy chain that ran along the side of what is called Penny Garth to which bulls were tied on bull sale day. What a sight that must have been, and what a mess there must have been in town after a big cattle or bull sale! In those days the animals were not sold by auctions; all transactions were made between dealers and individual farmers—a practice which left the farmer very much at a disadvantage.

Eventually some local men got together and tried to start an auction mart at the other end of the town. However, these early entrepreneurs found it difficult to break the dealers' grip on the buying and selling of stock. The man they sent through the town announcing that the auction was about to begin brought little response. Old customs die hard and the dealers had a well-established hold.

Timing, as always, is a vital factor. With the shortage of food and the high price of stock during the 1914–18 war, the time for the auction had come. Since it was a seller's market, the farmers readily turned to selling their stock by auction. The old method was gone forever and the bell the man had rung so desperately through the town to attract customers was used only at the mart to signal selling was about to start in the ring.

Today the prosperous market is an asset to the town and farmers and their families come from miles around. On market days visitors add to the crowds, which in their turn encourage stallholders whose wares fill every available space.

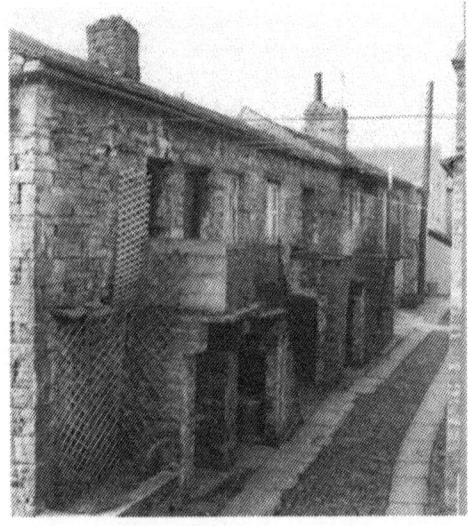

Behind the main street in Hawes, a ready-made film set,
complete with flags for the cartwheels.

6

Soon after we came to Hawes we applied for and obtained the catering license at the cattle market. This introduced us to the life of the farming community, and very interesting it turned out to be. On a quiet day there was always someone to chat to—sheep farmers from the 'out by' places, or dairy farmers and those who farmed a few acres in their spare time. Then, of course, there were dealers from all over the country. Truck drivers, too, were frequent customers because they had to wait about half the day to get a load and then work half the night delivering the stock, perhaps to the other end of the country.

We often listened to the old farmers' stories of their struggles. Although times were now good, old habits are not easily broken, and I didn't take it amiss when an old farmer bought a cup of tea, put in two big spoons of sugar, drank half of it, said he had spoilt it as he didn't usually take sugar, so would I fill up his cup? Of course, I always did!

I know there are a lot of jokes about these 'tight' old farmers, but one should remember these men are the survivors of that terrible farming slump which shook the agricultural world between the wars. After a year's care and hard work they would take their lambs to market and have to sell them for a few shillings each. I have great respect for these men who carried on and clung to their sturdy independence through those difficult days.

7

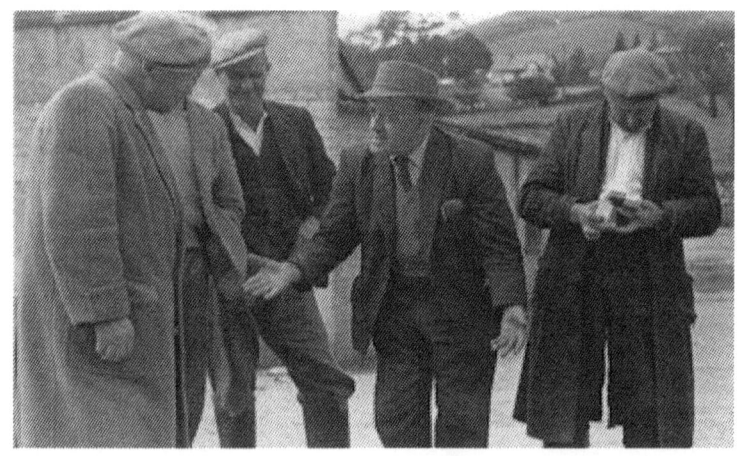

Mr McNaught—salesman

We have all stood and listened to the slick salesman at his market stall. They are all great salesmen who hold their audience. They have to, for their living depends on their success. At the cattle market we had Mr McNaught (I never knew his Christian name). Several times a year he would visit us from his native Glasgow to put on his show, sometimes in the ring, sometimes outside. Having laid out his wares, tools, stack sheets or any other wonderful bargains he had to offer, he started his patter. His listeners hung on to his words either skeptically or with amusement, as the case might be, while I made the most of the opportunity to grab a few candid photos of actor and audience.

Completely different was old Jim Smith from Clithero. He travelled by bus, arriving at the market on foot with his pack on his back. He was not a packman in the old sense of the word. (They tramped the countryside, pack on back, going from door to door with their goods, no doubt being as welcome for their bits of news as for their products.)

Jim sold waterproof leggings, a necessity for farmers, as well as the odd piece of second-hand clothing. He used to hang his stock on any convenient rail as near the ring as he could get. With a ready-made crowd at hand, he was ready for business. He was never short of friends to talk to, for he had become such a familiar figure over the years in a number of markets as to become an institution. The time came, nevertheless, when Jim gave up his round, and so another old character disappeared from the scene.

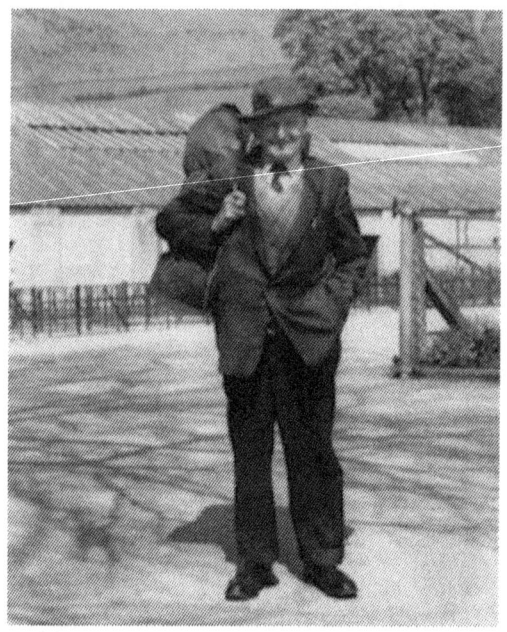

Jim Smith with his pack.

8

In these days of factory farming the attitude of farmers is often a subject of debate. I think back to the time when many made a living, however frugal it might have been, from a few acres. Some lingered on into the 'sixties and I particularly remember a brother and sister who had a very small smallholding with very few cattle—so few that each was named. When the time came for one of the tiny herd to go to market the lady would shed tears to see it go. Those were the times when they would come and ask me to take its photo—a memento of a lost friend.

9

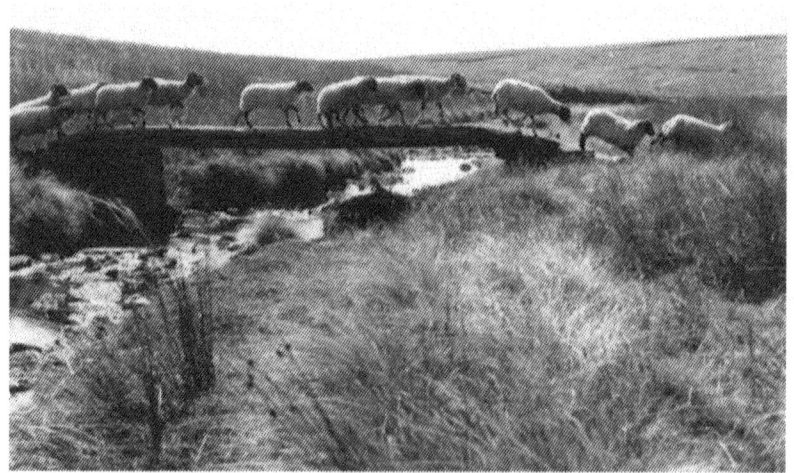

Home of the Swaledale sheep

Sheep and the dales cannot be separated. For hundreds of years, through good times and bad, sheep have been bound up in the economy of the dales. Either the meat or wool, or both, have formed a major part of the income of so many of the inhabitants. The very appearance of the fells and dales has been influenced and in parts dictated by the grazing habits of the sheep. Beside the streams at the close of the eighteenth and well into the nineteenth century, waterwheels supplied the power for many small mills for spinning and weaving wool in addition to that spun by hand. The dales knitters used a lot of this wool, and for many dales families this was a very welcome supplement to their incomes.

During the Second World War, when it was so important to utilise every acre of land in the country, the production of mutton from the fells was a valuable addition to the nation's larder.

The area where we lived is the home of the Swaledale sheep. The breeders are more than just enthusiasts; they're dedicated to their work that is at once their hobby and their life. They are great stockmen and real experts in their field. Breeding stock is selected only with the greatest care and consideration; but having once made his selection a farmer depends entirely on his knowledge and experience. I knew of a man once who sat twelve hours in the auction ring, watching 600 rams sold before the ram of his choice came into the ring—which he bought after 10 o'clock at night. That's confidence!

These men have a much-studied handbook, the Swaledale flock book. It's a hard-backed volume listing all the registered rams and their sires with photos of many of the winning rams from the previous year's sales. (The Swaledale Sheep breeders' Association issues it every year.) One year the Association was looking for an official photographer and, knowing that I was interested, the secretary offered me the post—one which I was delighted to accept and continued to hold for fourteen years.

Photographing sheep is a specialised job. In order to give me some experience, the secretary took me round many hill farms that summer, showing me the right way a sheep should stand and look to make a photograph that showed it off to its best advantage. Patience is the secret: not just a virtue, but a necessity—for the man holding the sheep, the photographer *and* the sheep! I found the animals from breeders who did a lot of showing were so used to the proceedings they already knew what to do, whereas a sheep that had had little handling could be a nightmare.

The ideal, of course, is to have the sheep standing free, which can take even more time—and film. However, a farmer friend had an ewe that had been overall champion at a number of shows and he wished to have its photo taken in its natural habitat—in the fells. We arranged to meet near the Butter Tubs, high on the fells between Wensleydale and Swaledale where there is nothing but open moor for miles around. He was waiting there with his Land Rover and I was amazed when, with the confidence of a lifetime's experience, he just turned the sheep loose. I had visions of it disappearing into the blue yonder, but I needn't have worried; two highly trained dogs placed the sheep where we wanted it and I had no trouble obtaining the picture we both had in mind.

At times I took photos of other breeds as well as Swaledales, and occasionally a farmer would bring a ram to our house where I would take it on the lawn. Eventually I arranged with a farmer to use his field. On one occasion a farmer from over twenty miles away won a championship at the Great Yorkshire Show. Since his ram hadn't been photographed on the show field, he brought it to *me*!

Today rams are not clipped before exhibiting in order to show off their wool. By July, however, it was getting past clipping time; consequently the wool had started to come loose and round the neck, in particular, it was beginning to look untidy. A farmer is difficult to beat when it comes to making do and mending, and so he produced some safety pins and did an instant camouflage job—not perfect, but all that could be done short of gluing the wool back on!

The Swaledale Sheep Breeders' Association hold their ram sales in October and it is then that most of the ram pictures are taken for the next year's flock book This was my job—to attend the sales at various markets and photograph the winners of the different classes or any ram which brought an exceptionally high price.

The Hawes sale occurs about the second week in October and is known not only by the farmers but the whole town as 'tup week.' All the high priced sheep and rams are sold then, the highlight of the week being 'shearling' day (now two days) with the record price going up every year. On this day even those who normally had no interest in farming whatsoever would ask me on one of my flying trips up town: 'What's the highest price?' or 'Has the champion been sold yet?'

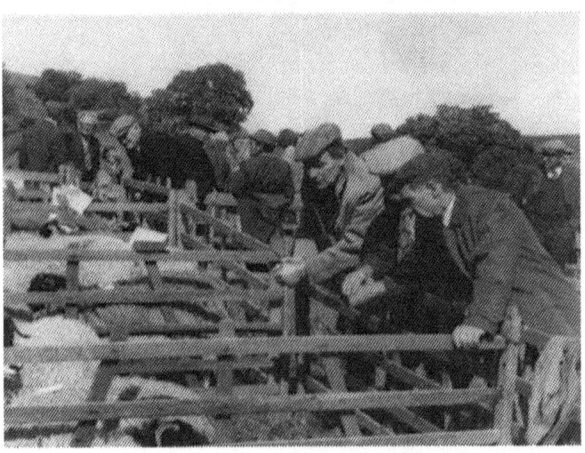

Sheep…their interest and life's work. At Muker show.

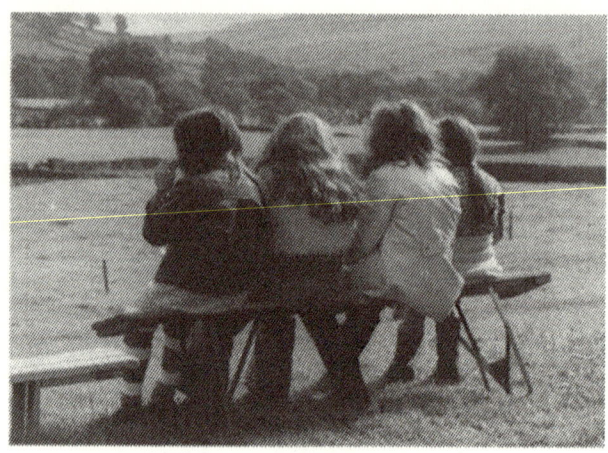

...to some, of course, there are other things. Also at Muker show.

10

By 7 a.m. on the big "tup day" the market is a hive of activity: there is an endless procession of Land-Rovers with their cargoes of tups, which are unloaded then guided or, if necessary, dragged to their respective pens. Once again, they are groomed and their faces are washed in whatever soap powder their owners fancy—a use of soap powder that I'm sure the manufacturers never envisaged.

When we took over the catering at the market in 1956, the top priced ram fetched a few hundred pounds. I remember the chief auctioneer saying it was his ambition to sell a ram for £1000. He achieved this and lived to sell a number well over that price. The last time I photographed rams at Hawes the top price was £14,000.

The sheep and ram sales were the busiest time of the year for us. We had to make much of the year's money in those few weeks. Tup week was the busiest week of all, when we were hard put to keep up with the enormous amount of food required. For a week we seemed to feed the whole of Swaledale and many more from far and near. To the sheep farmers, tup sales were their annual holiday. On these tup days, when they were not watching the sale in the ring, they would congregate round the pens and examine one anothers' animals in minute detail. These were long days, but their interest never seemed to wane as they divided their time between the ring, the pens and, of course, the canteen, to which I'm pleased to say they were frequent visitors; but wherever they were, their conversation centred on their favourite subject—tups.

The sales are catalogued, the starting number being drawn by ballot at the beginning of the day so that one has some idea when any particular animal is likely to be sold. When the time approaches for the champion to go into the ring the canteen would empty and the ring would fill to bursting point. The champion would enter and there would be a short speech from a market official who would then present the proud owner with a cup. The auctioneer would give the ram's pedigree with a good word for the breeder; then, for the first time that day, the chattering round the ring would subside as the bidding gathered momentum.

Meanwhile, the owner shepherds his ram gently round the ring, shaking his head if the bidding flags and saying "That was no good"—or he would make it "lucky," meaning there would be a good cash rebate for the buyer. Then, the hammer having finally fallen, the buzz of conversation would start again; the yardman would guide the star of the day into the buyer's pen and, once again, all the waiting enthusiasts would fall upon the champion and re-examine him for the umpteenth time.

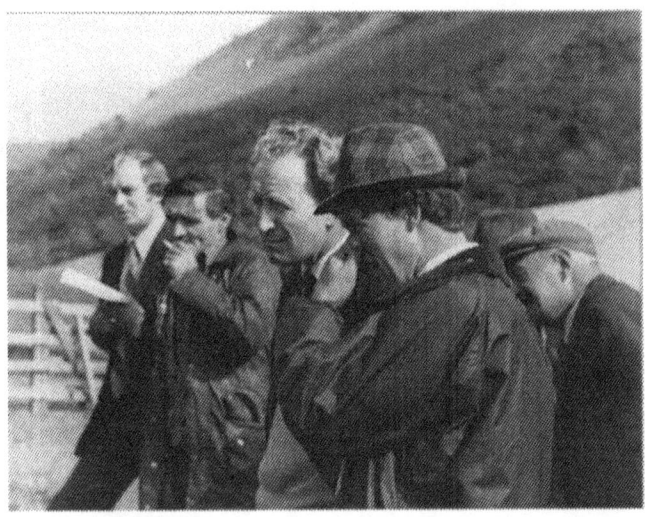

Judging—a very serious business.

Judging is a serious business, whether it is held in an auspicious gallery, a tent or—in the case of rams—in a field. With rams it's a very serious and professional business indeed. The whole proceeding is open to view and stretches across the field in a line of thirty rams or more, each held by its respective owner.

The line is whittled down to a dozen, and the remaining rams are examined and re-examined in great detail. They are turned loose a few at a time, then caught again while the judges stand back and consider them once more, apparently lost in thought. Meanwhile, the market officials glance nervously at their watches as sale time approaches. Nevertheless these men are not to be hurried by anyone. The whole line appears to be shuffled up and down, but all the time the winners are taking their place of first, second and third at the top of the line. Just as much trouble is taken in placing the fourth, fifth and sixth and highly commended—all very professional.

Having reached a decision with or without the help of the referee judge, the judges indicate the winners to an official hovering in the background with rosette ribbons in his pocket. He takes over, gets out his note book, takes down the sheep's number and owner's name which he probably knows already, and then it's the spectators' turn to have a detailed look at the winners.

My work now begins. Having found a place not too far for the farmer to drag his ram to, not too dirty for the animal to stand in, a position with a reasonable background where the photographer is not looking down on the sheep, we start to get the first ram in position.

Experience has taught me how the ram should stand. With words of encouragement, criticism and advice from the helpers and spectators, we pat his wool down here, fluff it up there and gently ease his feet into a position until he looks just right. Then, probably fed up with the whole business, the ram assumes a more comfortable stance and we start all over again.

The farmers are critics of photos as well as sheep, and advice given in setting up an animal is usually worth listening to. One can't tell an animal to stand still, so taking the picture was often a matter of split-second timing; so if the critics said "Now!" they were usually right!

I used to take the picture of the champion dairy cow at the annual dairy show that had to be taken in the ring. One year, as I maneuvered the cow round the ring to get it in the best position to show off its udder, with the market people fretting to get on with the sale and all the spectators taking a lively interest in the proceedings, I eventually got it right for that same split-second when a unanimous "Now!" went up from all round the ring. Luckily the flash worked!

11

The Hawes sports are held in June every year. The official title is the Hawes Athletic Society's Sports, but now horses do the entire running. The field is less than a mile out of town and within easy earshot of the loudspeakers. The starter of the trotting races can be plainly heard, ordering or pleading, depending on his degree of exasperation for the participants to get in order. He always had my sympathy because it's a running start! It must be difficult to space a number of running horses in their correct handicap

To see half a dozen horses tearing into a corner and pulling flimsy frames on cycle wheels, the horses' legs harnessed in a most peculiar manner, and a man balanced on each frame a few inches from a horse's tail, one might be forgiven if one thought that man and horse were heading for certain disaster. Miraculously there is no pile-up on the corner as these modern charioteers urge their horses on and speed down the straight, jockeying for position.

These are harness or trotting races. The whole idea of a trotting race is that a horse must lift up its legs and trot, not gallop. There is, of course, that curious harness between the horse's legs that is to remind it to do just that. This must be very difficult for the horse; a great deal of training must be done because, if a horse breaks into a gallop, it's immediately disqualified.

Girls drive alongside the men. They drive as well and as hard. I noticed, too, that they could hold their own in a verbal battle.

When a number of buggies—as they're called—bunch together, it says a lot for the drivers' skill that they don't collide. It would worry me that a horse would put it's hoof through the spokes of one of the buggy's wheels, and I see that the wheels are now fitted with discs which must remove this hazard.

There would be a line of ten or more bookies that always seemed to do a roaring trade as the crowd surged from watching one race to placing their bets on the next.

On a warm evening there was always a good crowd, for the occasion was always a meeting place for old friends. Crowds sat out on the bank and lined the track. The warmer it was the longer the queue was at the ice cream and pop stall, while the tent for stronger drink would be full to overflowing. After the heats were run it was often nearing dusk when it came to the final. I used to wait at the finishing post, hoping it wasn't too dark to capture the finish and winner in natural light.

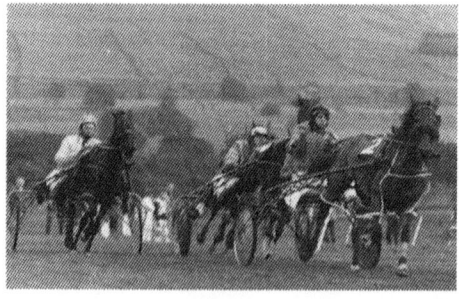

Harness racing at Hawes sports.

12

One of the features of the dales, along with the drystone walls, is the number of small barns scattered along the hillsides. In some dales there seems to be a barn to every two or three fields and many people wonder why this is so. I'm aware, from talking to farmers from the lusher, flatter lowlands, that these barns puzzle them, too; they used to wonder how it was possible for anyone on the hill farms to make a living at all.

Actually, these barns were a very practical way of adapting farming methods to circumstances and provided a solution to a number of problems. In the past the farms were all small, the work being done by hand and by the family; carting was done by horse-drawn sledge and any method that reduced the necessity for implements was a great advantage. Now, think how much easier it was when it came to hay time to have a barn accessible to every hay field!

The hay, having been first raked into 'windrows,' was swept up with an implement called a 'gate sweep' that was just like a five-barred gate laid flat. Pulled by a horse down the rows, this simple implement deposited large heaps of hay at the barn where it could be forked straight into the loft. This saved precious time and labour.

Underneath the hayloft are stalls for six or more cattle. With the hay conveniently stored above in the loft it was an easy matter to push it down to the cattle below—a saving of labour in winter. Having exhausted the hay in that barn, the farmer, if he had more barns, moved the cattle to another barn, thus taking the cattle to the hay instead of the hay to the cattle.

I remember well when hay timing not only involved a lot of hard handwork but was very complicated into the bargain. There were certain conventions, the hay having to go through a number of processes no matter what the weather, which made a difficult situation worse. What these old farmers would say if they saw modern methods of haymaking is beyond my imagination!

I've talked to old farmers who could remember the time in their young days when all the grass was cut by scythe. Some scythes were great six-foot blades and with their homemade strickles had an edge like a razor. This was the secret, of course: the sharper the blade, the easier the work, and the blade slid through the grass with a swish. The users of scythes today are called docking hackers. One old man told me that after a laborious day scything he would go to bed with the swish of the scythe imprinted on his mind and scythe all night.

13

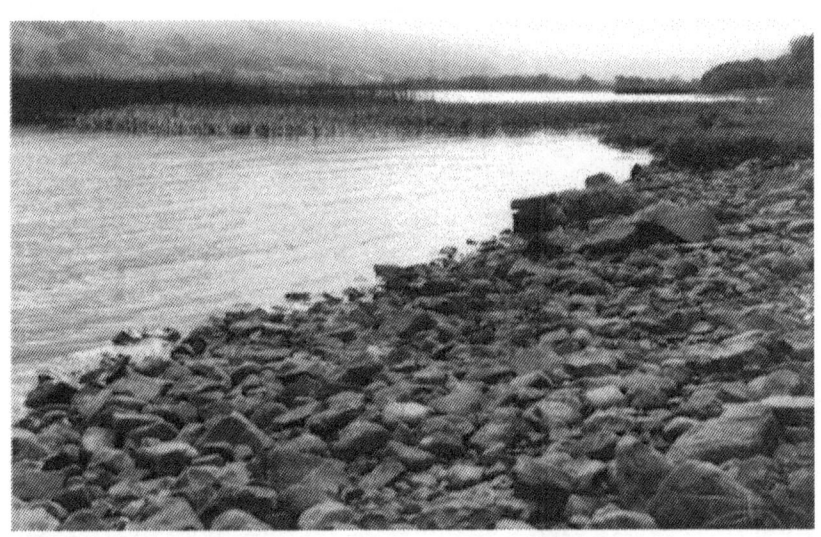

It was near here beside Lake Semmerwater that traces of
an Iron Age settlement and Neolithic arrowheads were found.

Semmerwater Lake is within easy reach of a number of towns, attracting more and more people interested in water sports. Every weekend these enthusiasts gather on the lakeshore, unload their boats from trailers and before long the lake is dotted with motorboats, sailing craft and water skiers.

High on the hillside at the southern end of the lake is the hamlet of Stalling Busk. The little church there is 'new,' having been built as recently as 1909. The ruins of the old church are down a steep and narrow path that runs towards the lake. One can detect that there was once a wall on either side of the path, making it very narrow: indeed, it must have been difficult for wedding parties if they took this route.

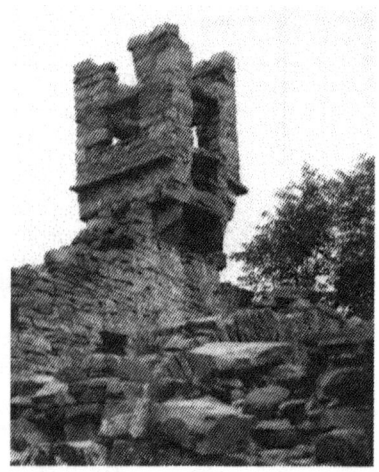

The remains of the bell tower in the ruins of the old Stalling Busk church,
not far from the shore of Lake Semmerwater.

The old church, as I said, is a ruin—for the second time. After being first built in 1603, it became a ruin before it had stood its first century. It was rebuilt in the eighteenth century, but by the early 1900's it was in a sorry state of repair. Indeed, it's said the roof had been patched so many times there wasn't a whole slate to be seen.

So the new church was built in 1909 and the old bell, which is thought to be even older than the first church, now rings from its new setting.

The tiny bell tower in the old church was still standing when I took my photos, but I've since heard it was blown down one stormy night. I'm thankful that at least I have a record of the old tower.

If you wander through the remains of this old building on a certain calm Sunday in August, you may well think that you've accidentally stepped through a time warp—when you hear the sound of a hymn drifting through the empty window. You may even think of the legendary drowned village below Semmerwater Lake.

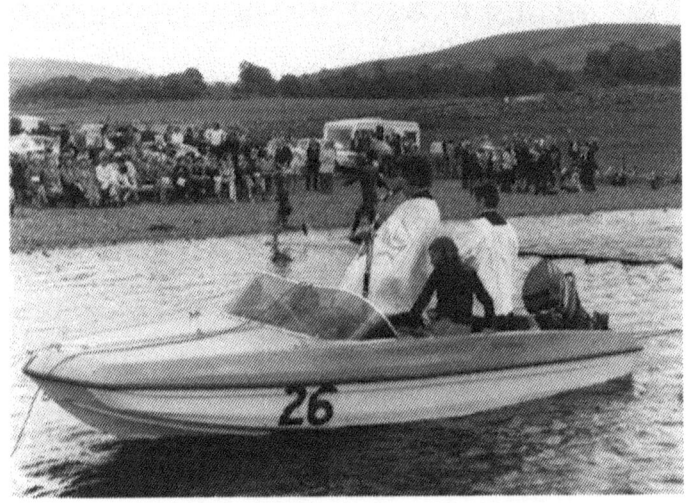

Rev. Malcolm Stonestreet, vicar of Askrigg conducts a service on the shore of Lake Semmerwater.

It is, however, the sound of a service that is conducted every year on the shore of the lake by the vicar of Askrigg. The little group of helpers who come with him set out a few rows of folding chairs and the Hawes band gets into position and begins to tune up. After the hymn sheets are handed round, the vicar takes his place in a boat moored at the little wooden jetty. When the service is about to begin the sound of motor boats, which filled the valley with their incessant buzzing, is stilled, and the sudden hush makes the most impressive opening that any service could have.

Semmerwater has links, too, with the more distant past. In 1937 the level of the lake was lowered to recover some of the land round the lake edge. It was found afterwards that on one part of the newly reclaimed shore there were the remains of what was some kind of platform that had been built on piles; also, there were iron fragments and other objects that proved it to have been an Iron Age site. Nearby Neolithic flint arrowheads were found, too, so this must have been a very old site indeed.

14

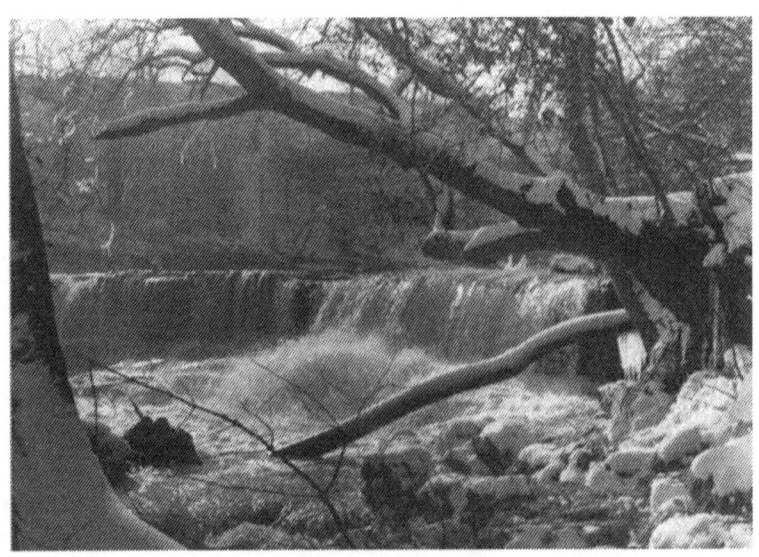

Aysgarth Middle falls in winter.

When we came to the dales in the 'fifties, there were very few visitors to be seen between October and Easter. If any of the summer visitors ever wondered what the dales were like in the winter, they certainly didn't come to see. Today, with so many owning cars that make the dales more accessible, and so many owning 'holiday cottages,' it stands to reason there are visitors all the year round.

During the time we lived at Hawes we saw all kinds of winters. Some were open with very little frost or snow. There were those, too, with bad snowstorms. Our altitude of over 800 feet ensured that the snow laid a lot longer than it did in the lower country down the dale. On the highest 'tops,' however, it could be much worse. In a bad winter the snow could lie, and sometimes did, from December to the approach of spring. This is a hard and worrying time for the sheep farmers. In a sudden blizzard sheep can be buried as they shelter behind walls or in the hollows and gullies with which the fells abound. Shepherding at these times is a feat of great endurance and to bring a flock through a severe winter to a safe lambing is a real achievement.

Sometimes the snow came suddenly in the night and we would get up next morning to a white and silent world with drifts across the door, while over the valley just the tops of the walls picked the pattern of the fields. At other times the snow crept slowly down Stag's Fell until it reached the snow line. There it would hesitate, as if saying "Shall I?" or "Shan't I?" Then the valley would quietly and gradually change from green to white. When there was no wind the snowflakes balanced on every twig and weighed the evergreen branches to the ground.

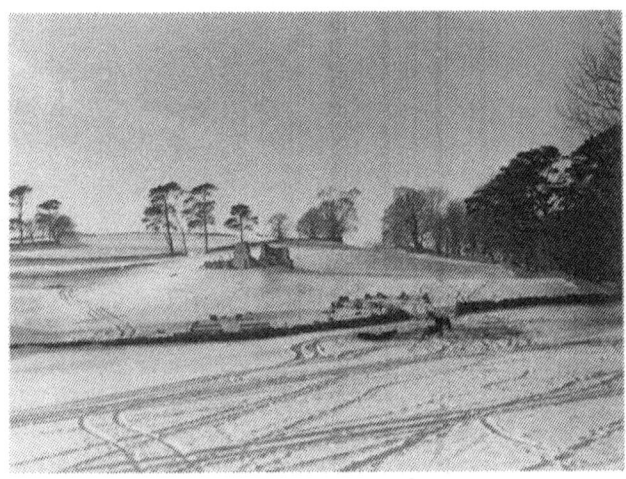

Tracks in the snow at Apperset.

In spite of blizzards, there were very few days in all the years we lived there that the buses didn't get through. The men with the snowploughs did a sterling job. If necessary they would work all night. Before snow ploughs were fixed to council lorries, the roads were kept clear by gangs of men digging with shovels—a much slower job. Remoter areas could be blocked for days and even weeks, but Hawes itself had a lifeline in those days—the railway. The trains always got through with supplies when the roads were blocked.

Snow cutting was done by anyone who cared to take part. If a man was laid off his usual work or was unemployed, or just wanted to earn a few extra pounds, it provided a useful opportunity. In a severe and prolonged spell of bad storms the roads could fill in nearly as fast as the men could dig them out. I've been told that in the terrible winter of '47–'48 some of the Wensleydale roads were dug out every day for weeks. In fact, it became difficult to find the original road because the walls were completely hidden under the snow. When the thaw came it was found that in one place the men with shovels had so completely lost the road that they were off course altogether into a field!

When there was a lot of snow we had quiet days with the catering at the market—not only because of poor travelling conditions but because the farmers had plenty to do at home, the snow making much extra work with the sheep. If the day before the market was fine and open we would lay in food for a normal day; then, if a storm came in the night, we would have a lot of wasted food. Gambling on the weather is a chancy business indeed. However, I made use of the time by going out to photograph snow scenes. I've forgotten about the lost lunches—but I still have those photographic records!

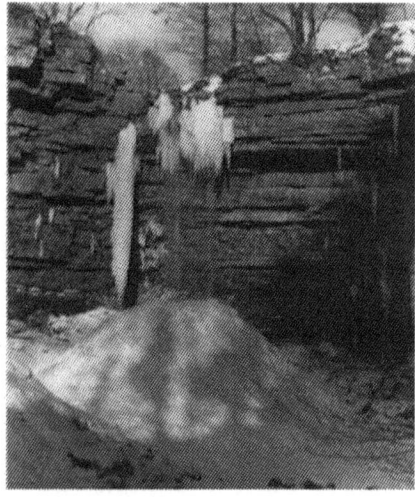

Hardrow waterfall frozen in the severe winter of 1963/64.

15

Before the days of tractors, hay balers and all the modern haymaking equipment, haymaking in the dales was a very hard and very often long affair. Only enough grass was cut out at a time which the available labour force (usually the family) could cope with; often the good weather just didn't last long enough, so it wasn't unusual for the hay time to drag on from late June to September.

Those farmers who could afford it hired Irish labourers. These came to the town on a certain market day and would hire themselves out for an agreed lump sum for a month or more as the case might be. If the weather was fine they were kept working all the hours they could; if the weather was bad and hampered haymaking, it was the farmer's loss.

In a wet year some of the hay was apt to be of very poor quality. This hay was usually fed to strong steers and came to be called 'bullock hay.' There's the story of an old lady who ran a small dales farm who was quite a character. One year she had an exceptionally good hay-time; every bit of hay was gathered in excellent condition (the weather must really have been exceptionally fine) and there was no 'bullock hay.' She was heard discussing hay-time with a neighbour when she burst into tears to confess that the hay was so good she had no 'bullock hay'! The neighbour who no doubt knew her very well was probably not so surprised as those who heard the story.

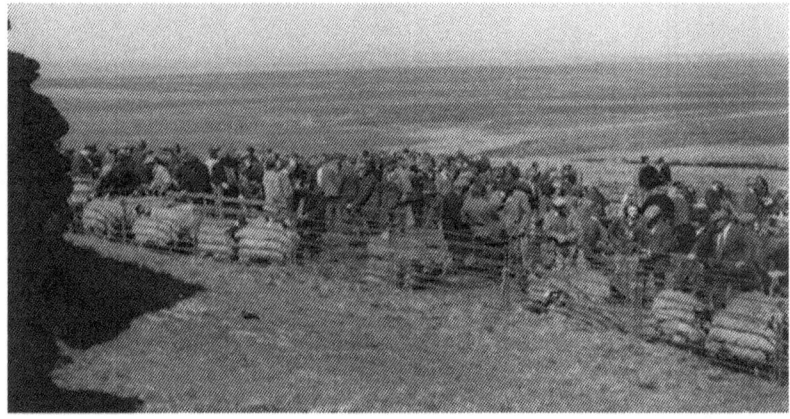

Tan Hill sheep show.

16

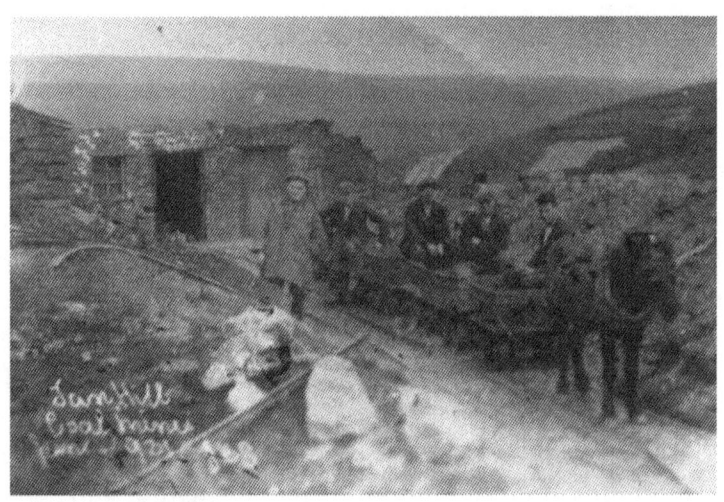

Old photo of the workers at Tan Hill coal mine.

A well-known landmark to tourists, the Tan Hill Inn, stands on the road from Arkengarthdale and Brough; or it can be approached through West Stonedale via a very steep hill from Keld in Swaledale. At 1732 feet above sea level it stands in splendid isolation, the highest Inn in England. Coal has been mined here for over 500 years and at times has supplied a lot of the country round about.

Drovers stayed here on their way between Scotland and the dales, and when the pony and horse sales were held at Brough Hill gypsies would frequent this out-of-the-way Inn. Whether any of the old tales told are true or not, it must have been a rough old place in those days. Then, too, in the days before rapid snow clearing, many a traveller would have had a wearisome stay when the place was cut off by snow.

It's a modern hostelry now and has a busy summer season, but the most important day is the Swaledale Sheep Breeders' show day. This is the first sheep show of the season and is held in May, followed by Reeth, Muker and winding up with the Moorcock. All the top and aspiring breeders exhibit here. To win a class is an honour. If, as can happen, a breeder produces a sheep that becomes a champion at all the shows, it's an honour indeed.

On a fine day it's a pleasant sight sitting on the great rocks behind the Inn that look over the moor towards Barnard Castle. Spectators study the sheep as closely as the judges; groups of farmers chatter, and the local band plays away on a makeshift bandstand—another day in Tan Hill's long history.

You will find the Moorcock Inn on the corner where you turn off the Hawes-Sedbergh road for the Mallerstang valley and Kirkby Stephen. Although there is only a pub and the odd cottage, you'll find it marked on most maps and it's a well-known landmark. It's not as high or as bleak and isolated as Tan Hill, but it's a lonely position and can be quite rough in winter. Here in September is the last rendezvous of the sheep men before the ram sales start the following month; but the Moorcock show ranks in prestige with any of the previous ones.

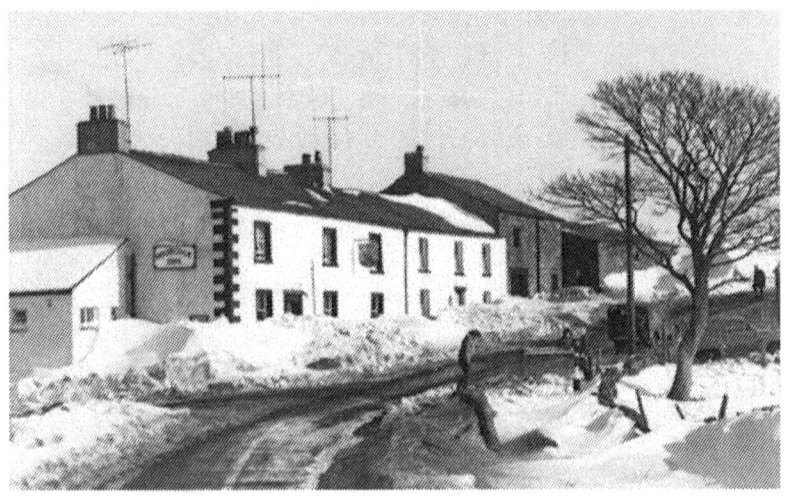

The Moorcock Inn in winter.

Every year just round the corner from the Inn, the organisers of the show mow about an acre of brown rushes ('seves' as they're known locally). They fence the plot in, then with wooden hurdles make a number of sheep pens behind the wall. At the end of the pens a few feet of this drystone wall is once again taken down to make the entrance and the show field is ready for business. The ladies of the district have a tent out of reach of the sheep in which they have an excellent display of cooking and handicrafts.

Looking at the prizes in the 1975 catalogue one can see that they were small even for the time; but it was the honour of winning that counted. With quite a few classes the first prize was £1, the second 50p and the third 25p. The challenge cups were of course the main target for which there was keen competition. A win here carried weight in the Swaledale sheep world.

Less than a mile up the road is the old Lunds School that has been closed for over thirty years. It's now used for a hall for the district and it was here a few years ago that the food was provided for the judges and officials of the show, all the food and crockery being brought from Hawes. The building has been completely unaltered and I'm pleased to say unchanged, even to the old earth closets in the corner of the old playground.

It used to be a long walk for all the children who came to this school from the scattered farms of the district, such as those who came from Mossdale three miles away. A man who had attended this school from Mossdale told me that he could remember his mother looking out of the door in the morning to see what the weather was like and, of course, he always hoped she would say it was too wet to go to school. Children also came over the fell from the now nearly deserted valley of Grisdale. In a bad winter these children must have missed a lot of school!

17

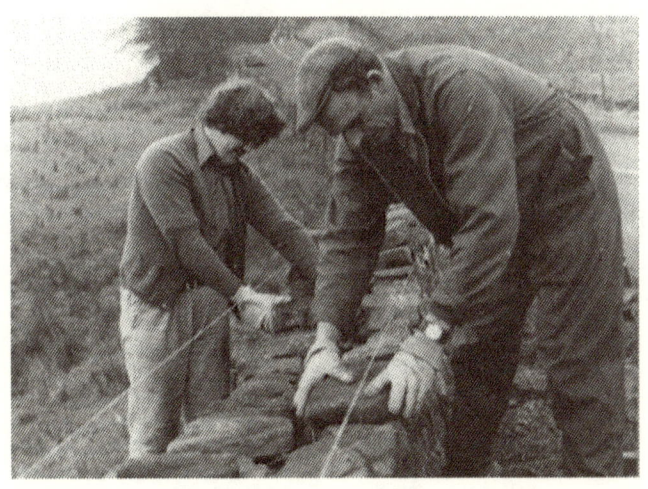

The skill in building a drystone wall is still alive.

The dales farmers are experts at drystone walling. They have to be because fell sheep are used to roaming free and take very badly to being fenced in—so they scramble over any wall in their way, knocking stones from the top of the wall where a gap soon develops, getting worse the longer it's left. Most flocks have one or two notorious 'jumpers' and, as the farmer knows the individuals of his flock as well as we know our neighbours, these are apt to go when it comes to a cull.

Consequently, drystone walling, unlike so many of the old country crafts, is a skill which is still very well known in the dales. Next time you come to a place where one of the dales roads has been straightened or widened, take note of the beautiful workmanship that has gone into the building of the new wall. A lot of the men who have done this work are men who have had farming experience. Some might still have a few acres on which to keep stock as a sideline and take pride in producing such good examples of their skill.

Many of the dales roads like the one to Sedburgh run between two walls, in some places going for some distance without being broken by a gate. This can create a problem for young curlews. Soon after they hatch they are remarkably good runners, but they are in that helpless stage when they can't fly. Sometimes they stray onto the road through a gate, then find themselves trapped because they can't find their way back. Here, apart from any other danger, they are at risk of being run over by passing cars.

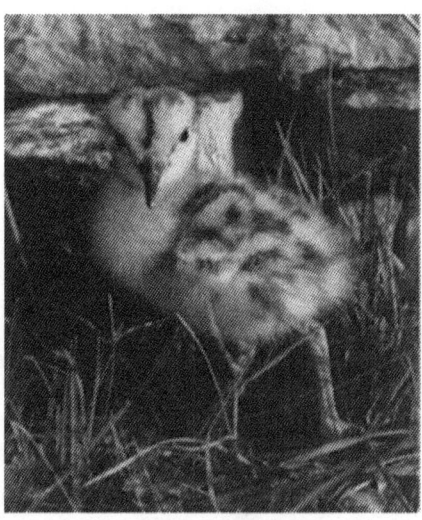

Young curlew rescued on the roadside on the way to Sedbergh.

I've often stopped and caught them, usually with great difficulty, and put them back in the fields. I've even snatched the odd photograph in doing so. One day I saw a young plover trapped like this on the road and it was having some trouble with it's running, the mother screaming wildly overhead. On catching it I found its legs were literally hoppled with sheep's wool. By the look of its swollen legs the wool must have been there for an uncomfortable time; it must have been a very relieved youngster that I released into the field after unravelling the tangled wool!

The making of shepherd's crooks is a craft that is becoming increasingly popular, the crook being a carved ram's horn. A lot of the carvings, some of them quite elaborate, are often very beautiful with their great detail they must have taken many hours of patient work to produce. There are sections in agricultural shows for these crooks and sticks; there is very keen competition and judging must be difficult. The makers all have their little secrets in processing the horns. Some use only British horns, some use horns from as far away as Australia. All must be soaked, boiled and processed in various ways before they finish up the required shape, each stick taking much time to complete. These craftsmen nearly always have a waiting list of orders.

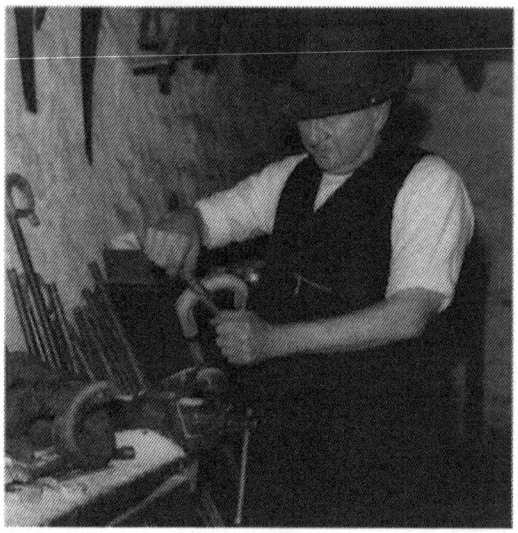

Mr Harker shapes a crook.

18

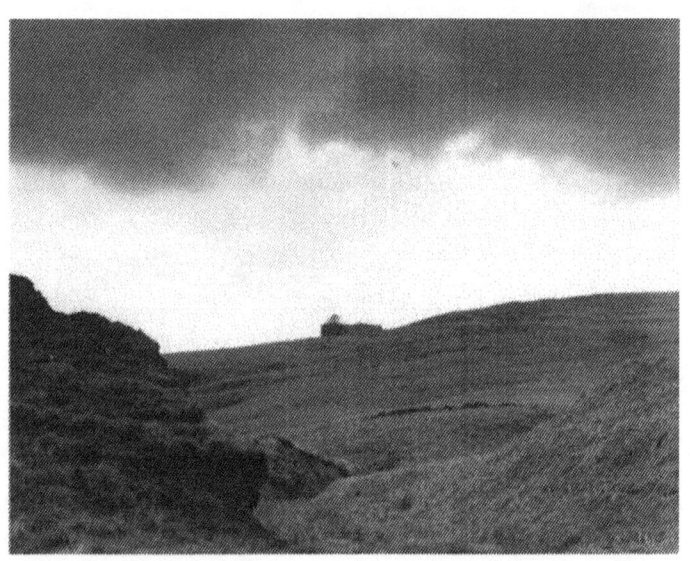

The bleak setting of Top Withens.

Charles Muller, a professor of English, had undertaken the task of editing *Wuthering Heights* for the use of students in Africa. He required a set of photographs of Haworth or anything pertaining to the Brontës. So one spring day we set off for the Brontë country. Crossing the moors of industrial Yorkshire, it came as a shock to me to see the change in colour of my familiar stone walls. They were black. I expected this in an industrial town, but not on the fells. The smoke is gone now but how long, I wonder, will it be before these walls lose their overcoat of soot?

Travelling south from Skipton we went up and down a switchback of lovely little dales. The walls on the moors might bear the reminder of smoking chimneys, but the fields were all a beautiful fresh green with the first flush of spring. We came down steep hills to narrow valleys with a stream at the bottom and, as sure as there was a stream there, there was a small mill. These were busy little dales once.

So many of these old mills have now been dismantled. In fact, a small industry has sprung up in disposing of the odd bits and pieces. The old bobbins have been ingeniously turned into such novelties as egg timers or skipping rope handles, while shuttles are widely sold for souvenirs in the tourist trade.

The Brontë parsonage sought by all Brontë pilgrims stands on the shoulder of the moors. It's approached by a very steep hill on three sides. The main street with its little cottages, cafes and gift shops is so steep that it looks as if each building is holding up its neighbour with its shoulder. What a pull it must have been for the horses in the days when the only horsepower had four legs—and it can't have been so good for the older inhabitants either.

Many visitors are no doubt disappointed to find that the church is new, but a tablet on the wall tells the whole tragic Brontë story that is a saga in itself. The rooms of the parsonage are unbelievably small. Walking round and looking at all the relics so carefully collected and displayed will, I expect, arouse many different feelings in the visitors. Personally, I confess to a feeling of sadness. It's a sad story, of course, but there is also the wonder that these Brontë sisters made such an impact in their short lives.

One of our main objectives was a visit to Top Withens. This is the remains of the house on the moor that, it is said, Emily Brontë had in mind when she wrote *Wuthering Heights*. It's a three-mile walk over a rough, twisting moorland path. In less than a mile one drops down into a tiny valley with a picturesque bridge composed of single slabs of stones stretched across a stream. It's a peaceful little spot and it's understandable why it was a favourite picnic place for the Brontë girls.

Above the valley is Top Withens that we could see on the horison. Eventually we reached what remained of the old house and found it to be an unexpectedly small place backing into the hillside for shelter. Only the walls were now standing and the roof was completely gone. The drystone wall that had fenced it in from the moor was now flat, the stones scattered, but a couple of lonely windswept trees were still standing there to defy the weather. Today it was warm and sunny but it wasn't difficult to imagine that on a day of lowering cloud or driving blizzard it would be a very grim place indeed.

I thought of the Brontë girls in their long dresses walking across the moor to this isolated house. On a fine day like this, did Emily sit on the fell and people this house in her mind with her own characters, then walk home to Haworth, her mind full of what she would write that night? Rather reluctantly we, too, turned to retrace our steps. But I was glad I had made that walk, for without it a pilgrimage to the Brontë country wouldn't have been complete.

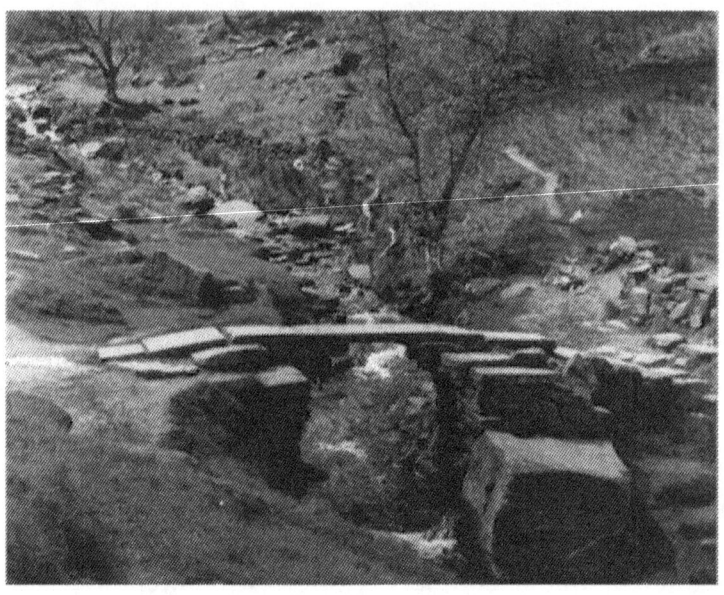

The favourite picnic place of the Brontë girls, on the way over the moors to Top Withens.

19

One of the most noticeable features of the Yorkshire dales is the outcropping strata of limestone running along the hillsides, sometimes repeated on the other side of the valley. The different strata form steps up the hillside with green terraces in-between. In the Ingleborough and Malham districts there are whole areas composed of nothing but lime-stone. These are the limestone pavements.

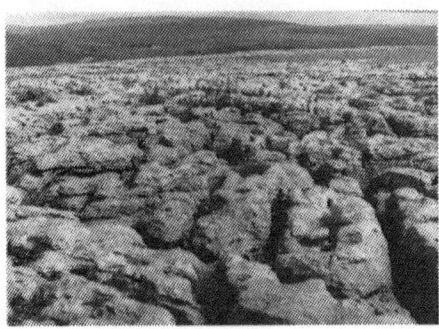

A limestone pavement.

When I stepped onto one of these it was like stepping onto another planet—just acres and acres of weatherworn limestone. The rock is criss-crossed with cracks and fissures, making a giant jigsaw worn smooth and rounded by the erosion of ages. Some of the cracks are a few feet deep, the sides lined with ferns and providing shelter for a surprising variety of wild flowers and plants that one wouldn't normally expect to find at this altitude. Not only is their survival helped by this friendly shelter, but by their inaccessibility from the ever-foraging sheep that nibble off the tops of plants as soon as they grow within reach.

I found one part of the pavement where a portion had been fenced off, and here there was a thriving wood with fissures so filled with vegetation that it was difficult to walk without putting one's foot down one of the cracks. The difference between this portion and the areas where the sheep had free access was astonishing and must illustrate how the grazing sheep have dominated this landscape for hundreds of years.

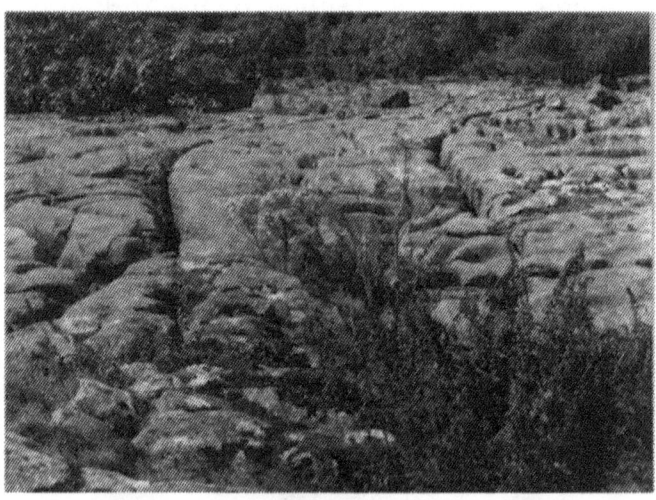

Over the wall where it is protected from the sheep the vegetation flourishes.

20

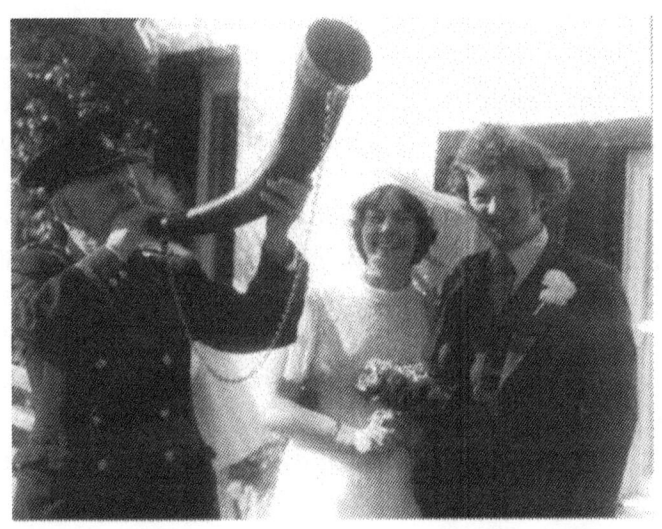

Bainbridge hornblower blows a blast for good luck at a local wedding.

Every country in the world has its wedding customs. There are many in England, the dales being no exception. Bainbridge has one of its own. Here it's the custom for the horn blower to meet the happy couple after the ceremony and sound the horn over their heads for good luck. In many of the dales villages it's the practice for the children to tie the church gates while the ceremony is in progress, so that the bride and groom arriving at the gates find them tied with yards and yards of string or anything else that occurs to the imagination of the children. The best man must then throw a few handfuls of coins, producing a mad but happy scramble, probably in the middle of the road for which any traffic must wait. If he has remembered to bring his penknife he can then cut the string. I used to bring my own—just to be on the safe side.

When I was a small boy in a Cambrian village I remember a certain wedding shortly to take place in which the young lady was to be married to a well-to-do farmer. The proud mother of the bride-to-be didn't want an unseemly scramble in front of the church gates, so she visited the school the day before the wedding and gave each child 6d. Perhaps it was less bother for most of us, but it wasn't as much fun.

Photographing weddings can be a permutation of problems. With most of the weddings I photographed there was only a very poor alternative to taking the pictures outside; consequently the weather was of great importance and I always hoped desperately for a fine day. I would settle for a dull day, even a cold day, although it was a problem if the bridesmaid's teeth were visibly chattering, or if the bride's insecure veil and head-dress took on a life of its own in a high wind. Finally, of course, there was the human element—that inexhaustible store of the unexpected, especially if there was a pageboy. However hot or cold, easy or testing, I was always very conscious that it was the bride's big day which could not be repeated and, I must confess, I was always relieved to hand over a successful set of photos.

Sometimes I would be asked to go to the bride's home to take a few preliminary shots of the bride and bridesmaids. Everything always seemed very well organised, the ladies having things well under control while the men stood round like spare parts. On one occasion, having arrived in good time, I set up my camera and waited for the bride who, I expect, was putting the final touches to her appearance. With ten minutes to go I was horrified to see the bride walk calmly upstairs in her ordinary clothes. But in an amazingly short time she came downstairs, looking spectacular in full apparel. I took the photo and she made the church no more than the customary two minutes' late. Surely that must qualify for any entry in the Guinness Book of Records!

The bridegrooms were often on the shy side. They would either come early, slipping into the church before I arrived, or try to walk past me incognito. Consequently, as soon as I saw two young fellows with flowers in their buttonholes, I would ask if one was the bridegroom— and if I had guessed right, would take their pictures. Once, however, I was standing chatting to the vicar in the church porch when two young men sporting carnations came up the path. As usual, I asked, "Which of you gentlemen is the bridegroom?" One of them looked puzzled for a moment and then asked, "Who's *that*?" I looked at the vicar and the vicar looked at me. "Well," I said, "if you're the man getting married today, that's *you*." That was all I could think of at the moment. But he confessed to being the man and the wedding proceeded as usual.

It's wonderful how these shy bridegrooms can change from being one of the boys to one of the great band of married men—and fathers. At one reception I attended the bridegroom was brought reluctantly from his friends at the bar to take his place beside his new bride; the next time I saw him, just over a year later when I called at his home to take the baby's photo, there he was—changing the baby's nappy in a most professional manner.

21

It was a lovely sunny Sunday afternoon when Myra and I went with friends to photograph some flowers near Widdle Head. We found the flowers and were on our way home when the sky clouded in very quickly and we were suddenly in the middle of a cloudburst. The water stood on the road. I had a job to see and we congratulated ourselves that we had made the car in time. A mile down the road, however, we ran out of the rain as quickly as we had run into it, and the road here was perfectly dry.

Now, there aren't a lot of people—even those who have lived in the dales all their lives—who have seen a wall of water come down the beck in a flash flood, so this seemed a good chance to actually photograph one. We pulled off the road and stood on a small bridge looking at Widdale beck that showed its normal summer flow. Using my usual black and white film I took a photo of the beck as it was over both sides of the bridge while Myra did the same in colour.

It seemed an awful long time in coming, but eventually it came—a foot or more of brown water right across the beck, seemingly riding on top of the quiet stream. We took photos again over both sides. It was an experience as well as a sight—and were we glad that we had our cameras!

A cloudburst on the fells where there is a very fast 'gather' can easily do this, but it's sheer luck to see one. There was one sunny market day I remember; everything was taking its usual course when someone happened to look over the valley towards Hardrow and saw the football field and the fields beside the Ure were all under water. All the farmers who had stock beside the river made the quickest exit from the market I've ever seen.

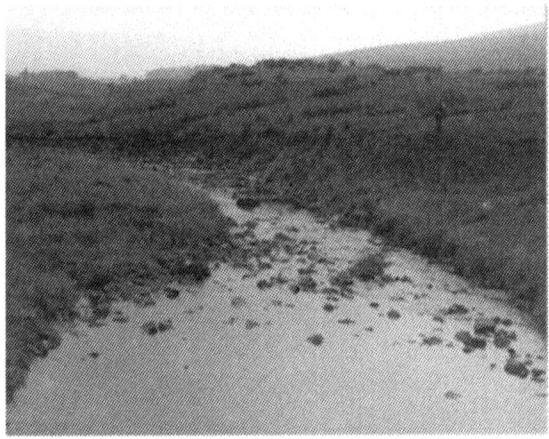

Widdle Beck before the flood; the tip of the flood can just be seen.

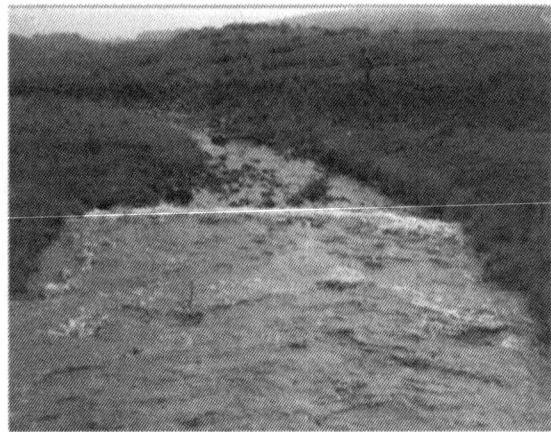

One minute later, the wall of water rides over the quiet stream.

22

It's astonishing how quickly all traces of a building can be lost. In the space of a hundred or two years whole villages and communities can just vanish and be forgotten. Bearing this in mind it didn't seem possible that the ruins of the small huts and compounds which I saw high on the terraces above the Yorkshire dales were indeed the settlements of a people who inhabited these fells in Roman times.

Although iron was still a scarce commodity, these people—the Brigantees—were coming into the Iron Age. In-between periods of uneasy peace their guerilla attacks were a continual thorn in the Roman's side. At one time they retreated to the summit of Ingleborough, protecting it with a great encircling wall. Eventually, however, they were defeated and those who didn't escape into the hills were taken as slaves, some to work in the lead mines near Nidderdale and Swaledale.

Here, on a site near Addleborough, are the ruins of huts in a remarkable state of preservation. They are mostly round huts. In some cases the lower parts of the wall still stand with other stones lying just where they fell. It needs little imagination to trace the small enclosures, the remains of the walls still marking out the jig-saw of tiny fields or folds surrounding the community.

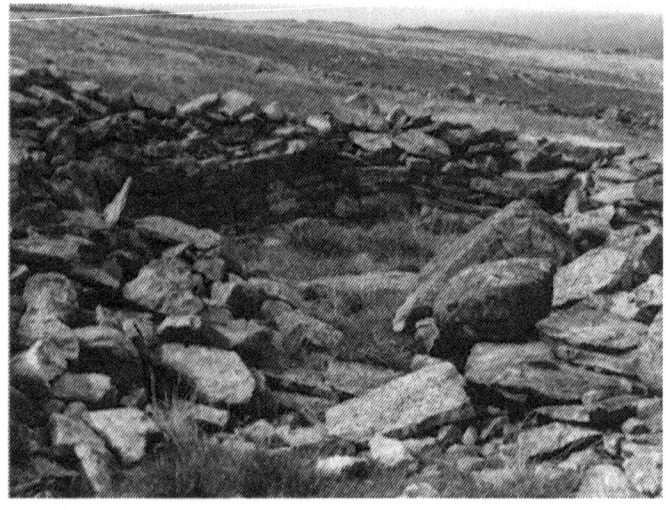

The stones just lie where they fell.

Looking over the site it seemed incredible that so much of Britain's history as a nation had been written while these stones had lain here undisturbed. On these sweet limestone pastures the sheep had seen to it that nothing was overgrown. No one had ever wanted to live here again, so it was only the shepherds who, with their successors on these fells who took a few stones in their turn to build their walls, who even slightly altered this scene since the old tenants moved on to pastures new, or perhaps fled from the Romans. As I came away I noticed a clump of nettles, a rare sight on the fell. I wondered if these, a sure sign of human habitation, could possibly be descendants of those long gone days.

23

There are quite a number of small, less well-known dales which have no through road, that are offshoots of the main valleys. Some of these dales are now almost deserted, the original small farms having all been joined to make two or three larger farms, with the spare farmhouses being let as summer cottages. They are lovely little dales. Very often the fields are less steep and the land looks at least as good as some of the more populous main dales. Perhaps it has something to do with not having a through road.

Some are still gated roads, but most now have cattle grids that are a great boon to all these out-of-the-way farms. It was certainly tedious to have to stop to open and shut two or perhaps more gates on every journey. That is how we feel now, but what of the days before the motorcar? If anyone wanted to go to the nearest village or town, he walked—unless he owned a horse and trap. Walking was taken for granted and there were many paths and short cuts saving miles on the way by road. So if one had to walk any distance, two miles or ten miles, it made little difference whether it was along a main valley or a small side valley. Consequently these places must have been regarded in a different light than we do today.

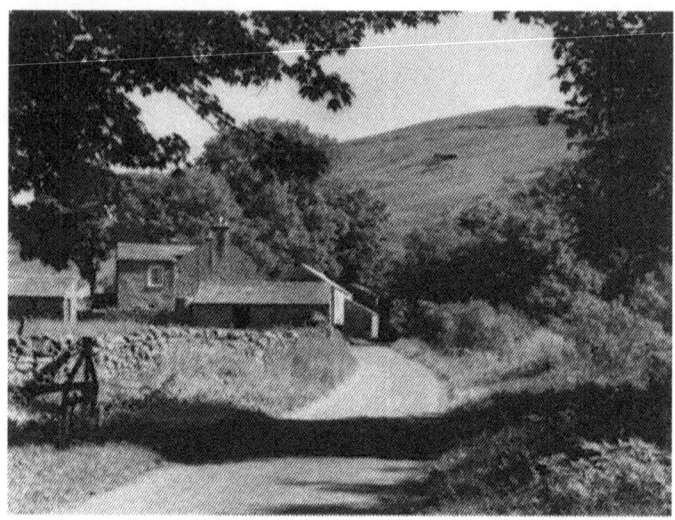

Cotterdale village.

Less than three miles on the way from Hawes to Sedburgh there is a turning on the right which will take you to Cotterdale. This is one of those secluded little dales. The road runs through open fields before dropping down to run beside Cotter beck, revealing a dale with a much flatter valley floor than, say, the more populated valley of Garsdale just over the hill. Two miles or less, and there is the tiny village of Cotterdale with its own little chapel and few houses straggling beside the Cotter beck.

Stories of the dales knitters have been well documented. Whole families joined in, men, women and children. They even knitted as they walked to tend their livestock, while neighbours would gather together and in the dusk would poke the fire to make a blaze when there was a dropped stitch.

All stories improve with the telling and grow with the years, but the story is still told of the lady who lived in Cotterdale who could knit a pair of stockings (I don't know how big) as she walked the three or four miles to Hawes and back. Now the only people who walk from Cotterdale are those who walk for pleasure, a pastime that is becoming more popular every year. It's recorded that Lady Anne Clifford made a perilous journey in a coach over what is now called Cotter Riggs, something, she claimed, that had never been done before, and I doubt very much whether it has been done since.

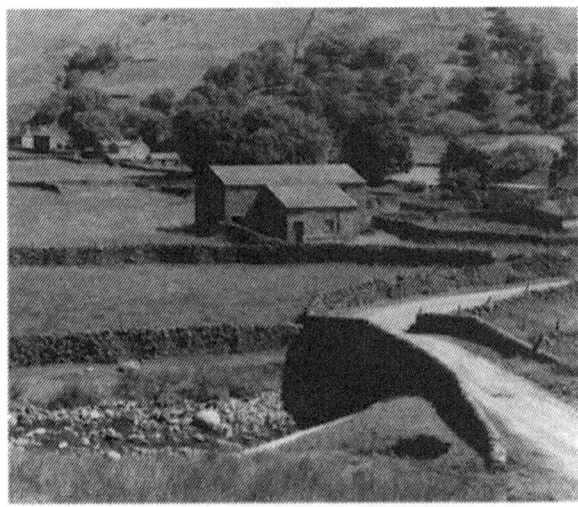

The peaceful setting of Cotterdale village.

24

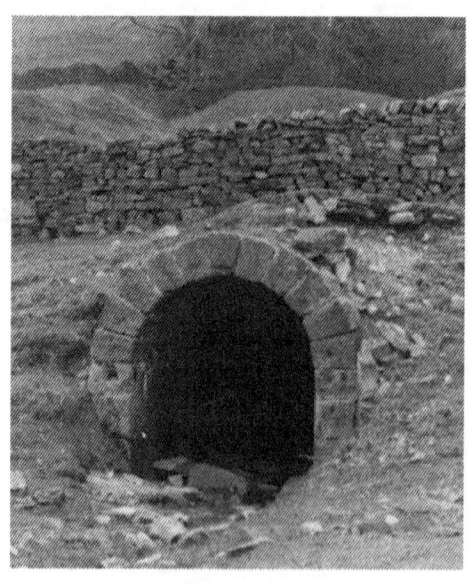

Entrance to a drift mine.

For centuries lead mining has been carried on in these dales. The traces aren't difficult to find—old buildings, now ruins, great gashes in the hillside, old spoil heaps and the entrances to old drifts, tunnels still beautifully arched in stone but very dangerous to enter. If you look at the 0.5. map of Swaledale, it's soon apparent that the fells are positively peppered with old mine shafts—a hazard to the unwary walker.

Some of the ruined buildings are the remains of old smelt mills. The mill would be situated in a valley bottom near a plentiful supply of water. Here one can often see from the ruins of the mill the broken-down remnants of a tunnel, stretching up the hillside, half above and half below the surface—turfed over originally, but now fallen in in many places and looking like the work of an outsize mole that kept coming up for air. These were the smelt mill chimneys and were a very simple way of not only providing a chimney but taking the smoke and fumes to the top of the fell where there were only sheep. What affect it had on the sheep I have no idea.

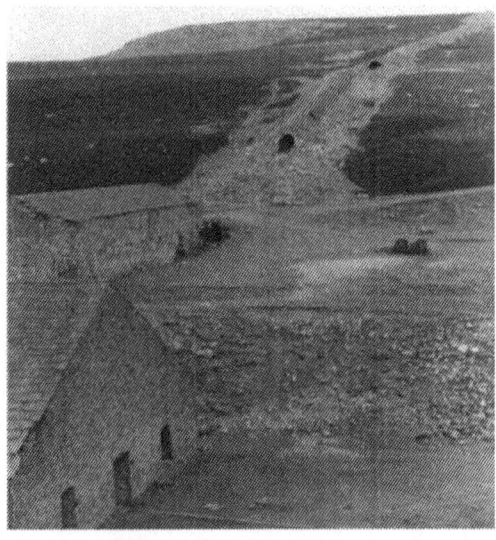

Lead smelt mill chimney.

There was a rather unusual chimney at Rookhope, a mining village three miles from the main Weardale valley. The smelt mill stood beside Bolts Burn but was a hundred yards or so from the fell proper, the road to Allenheads running in-between. The London Lead Company that owned the mines in the area surmounted the problem by leading the chimney over the road in a covered viaduct, then straight up the fell.

Years ago I was told by old Rookhope miners that the chimney was cleaned by damming some water on the fell—water which was then simply turned down the chimney to flush it out. I've been unable to verify the story that a man was once caught in the flood and drowned. However, just to work in a smelt mill in those days would be an unhealthy job.

In the last century many lead miners worked smallholdings; by an unusual method of shift work they managed both jobs very well. It enabled some who worked at Rookhope, for instance, to live up to twenty miles away, such as at Alston Moor. The system worked as follows.

Early Monday morning, with three days' food packed, the miner would leave his wife to look after the smallholding and walk to the mine. At the mine there were buildings called 'shops'—buildings specially laid aside for the purpose where he could sleep and prepare his food between shifts. He would proceed to work eight hours on and eight hours off, so that by Wednesday he had completed a week's stint of shifts.

Mining thus finished for the week, he would walk home to his smallholding where the open air was a much healthier occupation than mining—and only a man who has worked underground all day knows how sweet the open air smells!

25

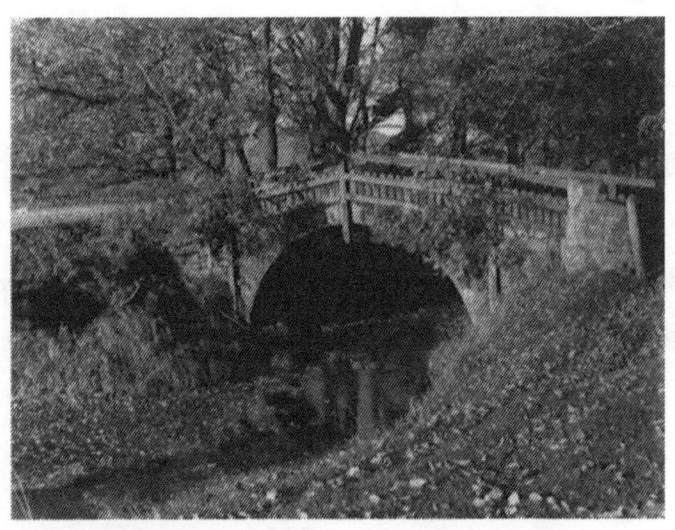

Lovely example of a packhorse bridge at Hawes.

For hundreds of years the only way to transport the lead was by packhorse. Packhorse bridges can still be seen throughout the dales; so are packhorse trails, if you know where to look. Sometimes beside the road over the open fell you can see what looks like an overgrown water course or even two or three running parallel, two feet or more deep but running up hill and down like no watercourse ever did. These are the remains of the old packhorse trails. If one became too muddy they simply moved over and made another track.

The Romans worked these mines. When they vanquished the Brigantes, the tribe that inhabited these hills, they took many as slaves to work in the mines. It's interesting to read that 'pigs' of lead were found beside these tracks, inscribed as coming from the silver mines of Brigantia A.D. 81–82. One, inscribed from the time of Hadrian, was found on the moor in Swaledale some way from the track. Lost or stolen, it lay there for hundreds of years, usefully dated—a Roman habit which has been such a help to historians.

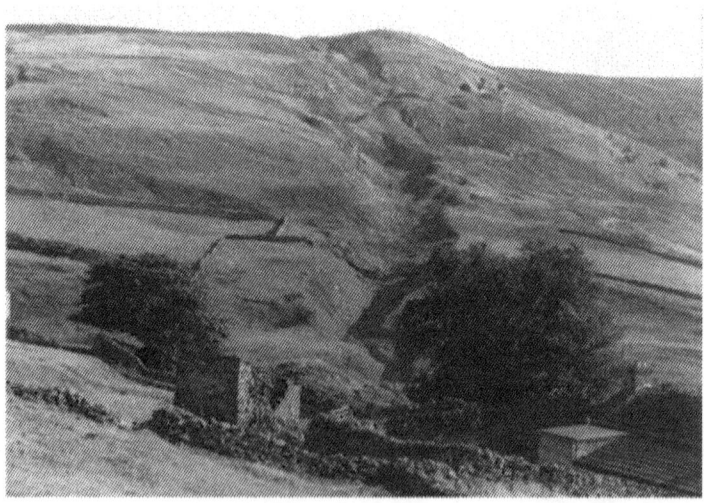

The 'Hush' at Booze.

There is something either sad or romantic about a deserted village, depending on how it strikes you. Perched on the hillside off Arkengarthdale there is a nearly deserted mining village with the very evocative name of Booze. Approached by a steep, very twisting and extremely narrow road, there are two or three holiday cottages and a farm among the ruins of Booze. The old stone water trough stands empty beside the track while among the rubble of a once inhabited home a few gooseberry bushes survive in what was once a garden.

Across the valley, from the top of the fell to the bottom and continuing up this side of the valley and through the village to vanish into the fell, is a great 'V' of an outsize and overgrown ditch. It's what is known as a 'hush.' Years ago when a lead vein was found exposed, in order to uncover as much as possible with the minimum of effort, the top cover was removed and, if water was available at a higher level, it was dammed and then released down the hillside, exposing more of the vein as it went.

I've read the accounts of two local historians who visited Booze in the last century and both complained bitterly that there was no pub in the village—which was perhaps the final irony.

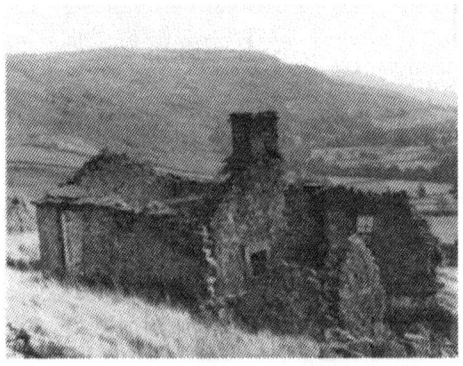

View over the ruins of Booze.

26

Hardrow is just a hamlet, but a well-known landmark of the dales because of its waterfall—the highest unbroken waterfall in England. Once Hardrow had another claim to fame—the Hardrow band contest. To win at Hardrow was one of the steps on the way to the top band prizes.

In the days before cars and buses, excursion trains were run to Hawes station; the sidings were jammed full with the overflow carriages parked in sidings down the dale, while hundreds of visitors made their way on foot across the fields to Hardrow.

In 1976 the contest was restarted after many years and is now held in May every year. Today, instead of sidings full of trains, there are fields full of cars. The contest is held at the entrance to the gorge that leads to the waterfall. It's a natural amphitheatre; the terraces that long ago were cut into the hillside for seats are still there, while on the level stretch beside Hardrow beck the old stone bandstand is in use once more.

The bands are numbered; the numbers are drawn one by one and they take their place on the stand. Meanwhile in a small closed tent nearby the adjudicator sits and awards his marks. Eventually, at the end of a long day, he emerges to announce the number of the winning band and the runners-up who no doubt hope for a better performance next year.

This is a truly wonderful setting; when, at the close of the contest, the massed bands play a few old favourites, the atmosphere is fantastic and one appreciates the vision of those who had the imagination and the faith to make their dreams a reality.

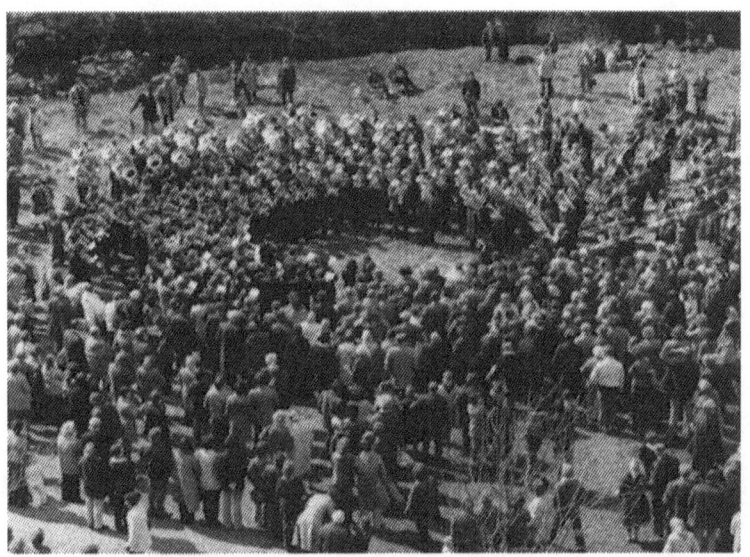

Massed bands at the conclusion of the Hardrow band contest.

27

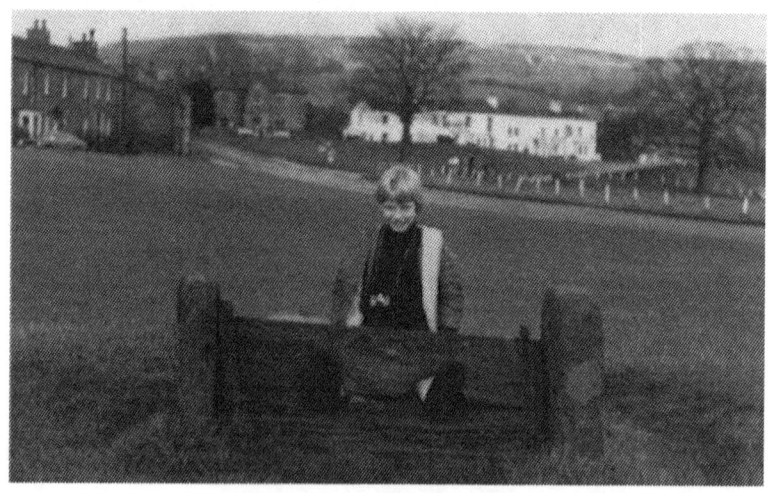

In the stocks at Bainbridge!

Bambridge, one of Wensleydale's picturesque villages, is well known for its extensive greens, its stocks in which hundreds of visitors take one another's' photos every year, and its horn-blower. In the thirteenth century Bainbridge was on the edge of the forest of Wensleydale, when the custom was established to blow a horn every evening to guide travellers out of the forest before nightfall.

An old horn dating far back was used until the last century when a smart new horn, complete with silver chain, was introduced. This now hangs on the wall in the Rose and Crown across the green. For generations blowing the horn was the duty of the Metcalfe family. It still is to this day because, when old Jack Metcalfe died in 1982, the duty was taken over by his great nephew, Alister Metcalfe, who hadn't even reached his teens.

For over thirty years Jack Metcalfe had faithfully taken down the horn from its place in the Rose and Crown and blown a blast over the trim greens of Bainbridge, if not for the benefit of the lost travellers in the forest now long gone, then at least for the delight of the modern travellers who flock to the dales in ever-increasing numbers.

What a different sight it must have been when a horn was first blown those hundreds of years ago. I wonder if there was any trace of the Roman fort that stood on the hill just over the shortest river in England, the Bain. That fort would have seen plenty of action in its time; in fact, it was attacked and burnt down more than once. A gentleman once suggested that the legendary lost Roman legion was on its way to relieve this hard-pressed outpost when it vanished into history. Just an idea, perhaps, but then a mystery always breeds theories so you take your pick—or try to keep an open mind!

28

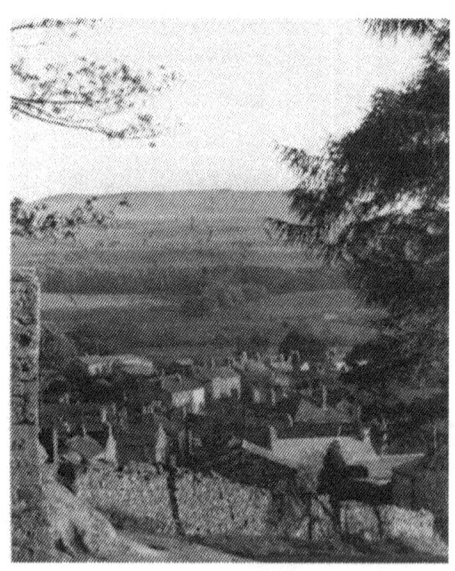

Askrigg from the Swaledale road.

The village of Askrigg once had a market, but that lapsed long ago. The old market cross still stands, though in the middle of a cobbled space outside the church gates—as does the bull ring set firmly among the cobbles nearby. Once the village was well known for its clock makers. Grandfather clocks (or long-faced clocks as they are often called) inscribed with the maker's name and Askrigg come up from time to time in antique sales and now fetch prices that would astound their makers.

Today Askrigg is well known as the setting for parts of the TV series *All creatures great and small.* The vet's house in the film is here while the series itself was filmed all round the neighbouring dales, much to the interest of everyone in the area. Abbyfield Trust, which does much for the elderly, bought this house and the casts of *All creatures great and small* and *Flesh and Blood* (much of which was filmed in Weardale) organised a charity cricket match to help with its purchase. Actually £6000 was raised. I don't normally have the opportunity to photograph such well-known celebrities and to do so when they were in the holiday mood in which they played the match was a pleasure indeed.

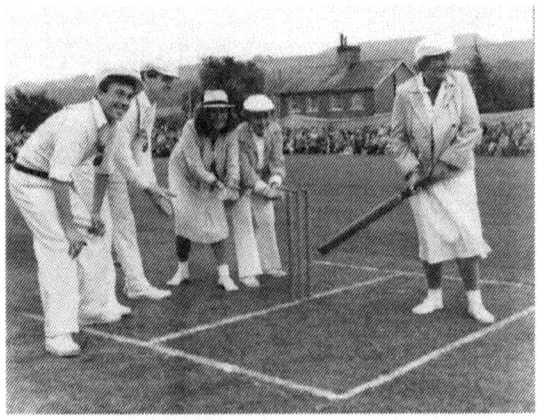

The casts from All creatures great and small and Flesh and blood play a charity cricket match at Askrigg.

29

By 1968 the old line from Hawes to the Carlisle-Settle railway at Garsdale junction was gone. So, too, had the steam trains. However, much to the delight of hundreds of steam enthusiasts throughout the country a 'last' steam train was to be run on the Carlisle-Settle railway and the train, packed with enthusiasts, was due to stop at Aisgill summit.

Aisgill is only a matter of about seven miles from Hawes, so Myra and I set off that Sunday afternoon to take some photos. The summit is about two miles from the Moorcock on the Kirkby Stephen road. After the Moorcock we began to come across cars parked closer and closer together until, when we reached the place where the train was to stop, it was only with great difficulty that we were able to edge our Mini onto the fell.

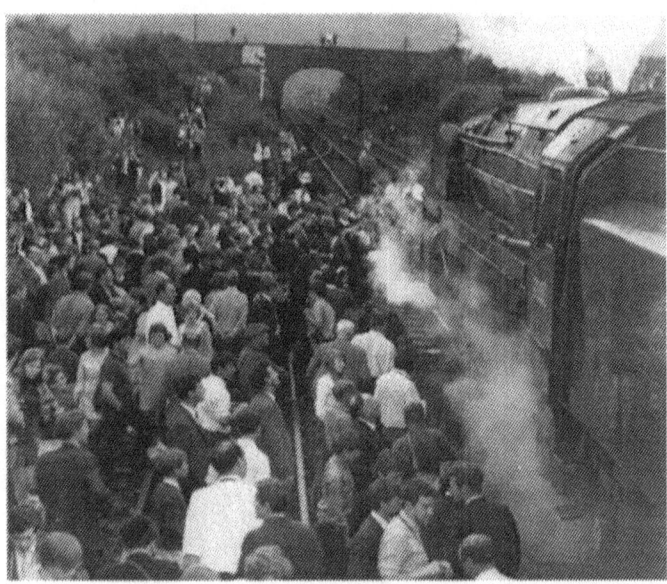

The crowd poured onto the track.

We were amazed to see the enormous crowd gathered everywhere within sight of the track. It was our first experience of meeting these keen steam folk and we were astounded on talking to some of them to find they came from all over the country, even as far afield as Cornwall.

Hundreds of cameras clicked when the Oliver Cromwell came into view and stopped beside the signal box. Against every regulation the railway company ever made, the crowd poured down onto the track and besieged the train from all sides. We, too, got busy with our cameras just like everyone else. I've never seen so many cameras.

Meanwhile the celebrity stood there, gently puffing steam while the 'Undertaker' who accompanies a last run stood there in his top hat and tails, solemnly surveying the surging crowd. The time came for the Oliver Cromwell to resume its journey and, as quickly as they came forward, the crowd left the tracks and made their way up the bank and over the fence—another piece of history well and truly recorded. Myra's record was much better than mine and one of the photos included here is hers.

I've said that the crowd left the track quickly, but it was the last thing they did quickly for some time. During the last half hour, while we were waiting for the train to appear, cars had parked on both sides of the narrow road for a mile or two either way and the token number of police were unable to cope with the resulting jam. Everyone did the only thing they could and waited for the head of the queue to move off.

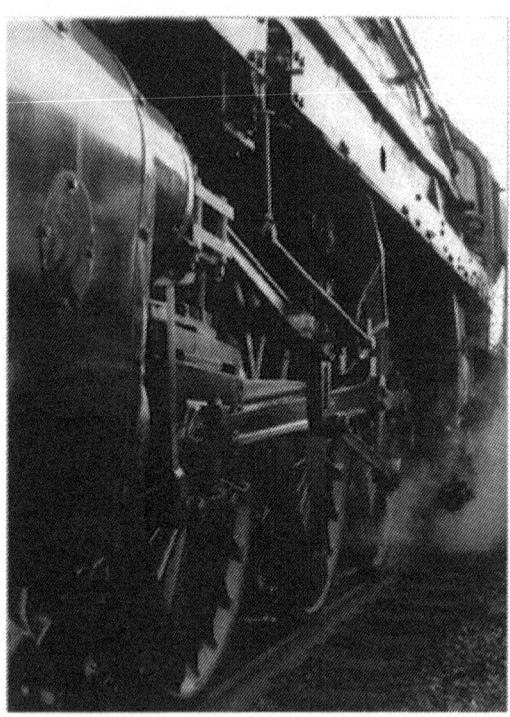

The driving wheels of the Oliver Cromwell.
(Photographed by Myra Moore.)

30

A mile or so along the road that runs from the Moorcock to Kirkby Stephen is a road that turns off to the right and goes downhill through a plantation. On the wall at the entrance of the plantation is a Youth Hostel sign, probably seen with relief to many a tired walker. He or she, however, would need to take another deep breath because the hostel is yet another mile up the other steep side of the valley.

Half way to the hostel in the bottom of the valley is the young Ure. Cross it by the ford or the little foot bridge and there, in the middle of a small field, is Lunds church—a simple little building that blends into its lonely background. At the time I first saw it in the late 'sixties it was in good repair, the inside beautifully kept and full of a quiet peace. Since then it has gone through times of great neglect, having fallen into such bad repair that snow has been known to lie on the floor and seats. Legend has it that there was once no door, the doorway being blocked by a thorn bush to keep out the cattle so that the last of the congregation to leave would replace the thorn in the gap.

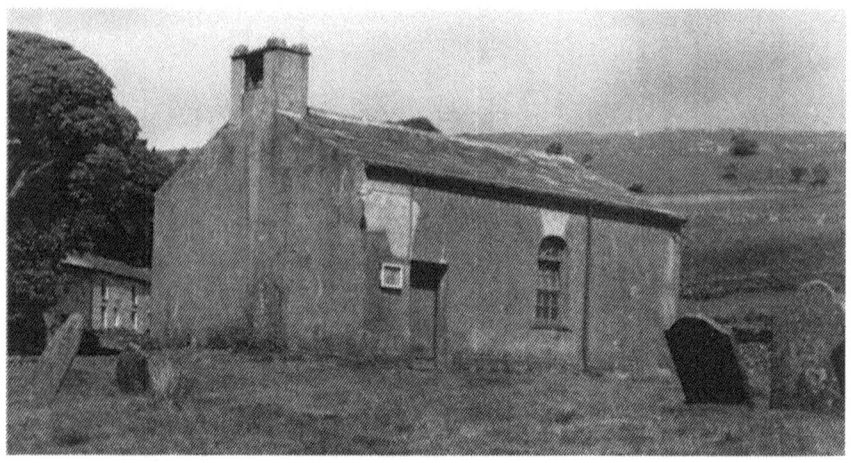

Lunds church.

Hellgill waterfall can be seen plainly from the road to Kirkby Stephen and is quite a sight after heavy rain. Beyond, way up the hillside, are the sources of both the Ure and Eden; close together here though one joins the sea in the East and the other in the West. It may not be a fact that Dick Turpin made a spectacular leap over the river up here, but it *is* a fact that Lady Anne Clifford used to follow a track along this mountain side on her way between Pendragon Castle and Cotterdale; there is a record that she was so impressed with Hellgill bridge that she sent her nephew to have a look at it for himself.

After Hellgill we enter Mallerstang and in a few miles come to Pendragon Castle—a name to conjure with! Leaving aside any legendary claims, the castle has had a long and chequered history. Twice it was burnt down by the Scots and eventually rebuilt for the last time in 1660 by Lady Anne Clifford who, having seen it as a ruin when she was a girl, dreamed of one day having it restored. She rebuilt Brough Castle too, improving the lesser properties on her estate and contributing generously to the repair and sometimes rebuilding of a number of churches, helping not only with hard cash, but in material such as lead from her own mines.

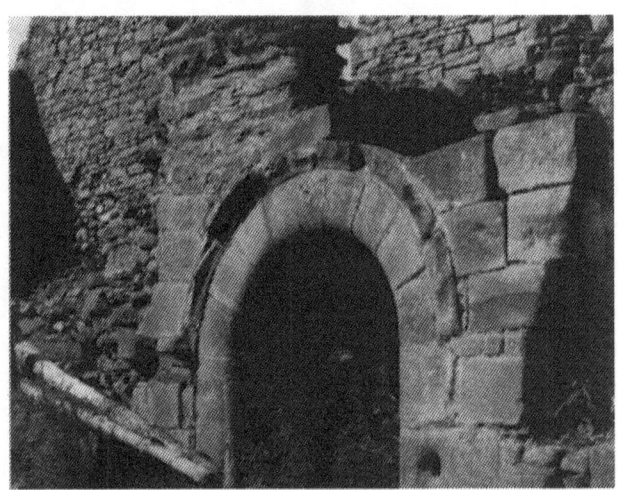

A beautiful arch among the ruins of Pendragon Castle.

One of the rebuilt churches is the twelfth-century church of St. Ninians near Lady Anne Clifford's mother's home at Brougham Castle. Nearly two miles through a number of fields along a cart track, it stands surrounded by its little graveyard in the centre of a large field. Her initials and date are inside the church in plaster relief at the East end and it's quite believable that the church is very much as she restored it, down to the family pews with their little doors looking as if she only walked out yesterday.

On various photographic projects I took photos from Appleby in the North to Skipton in the South. In so doing I repeatedly came across the name of Lady Anne Clifford, her journeys running like a thread through so many of the dales. She spent a lot of time travelling between her castles. Many times she made the journey between Appleby and Skipton and, of course, travelling in those days was a major undertaking. A whole retinue of servants went with her, taking tapestries, curtains, bedding and a huge amount of household necessities in a convoy from castle to castle. For a cavalcade like this, of coaches and other wheeled vehicles, to travel over rough tracks that couldn't be called roads must have made each journey something of an expedition.

Pendragon Castle would be her first port of call from Appleby, which was probably one of the easiest stages. The way would then be hard along the side of the fell through Mallerstang and on to Mr Colby's house, Colby Hall near Askrigg, or perhaps Nappa Hall on the other side of Askrigg. This was the ancestral home of the Metcalfes, the most famous and populous family in Wensleydale. When Sir Christopher Metcalfe was High Sheriff in 1558 he was said to have attended York Assizes at the head of 300 mounted followers consisting of his own family or important tenants.

Nappa Hall, a castellated farmhouse of the fifteenth century, is still occupied, as is Colby Hall, although this is now divided into several dwellings. From one of these Lady Anne would set off on perhaps the roughest part of her journey. It was over Stake Moss. There is a track, part green road and partly a road of large loose stones, which takes off over the fell from the road that runs from Bainbridge to Stalling Busk. It's a bad track now; but even in those days, up steep banks and over open moor with wheeled vehicles, what a test it must have been—a really hazardous undertaking in bad weather.

After the moor the drop down to Buckden would present a whole new set of problems to anything on wheels. This journey she persisted in making to an advanced age, travelling when necessary by horse litter.

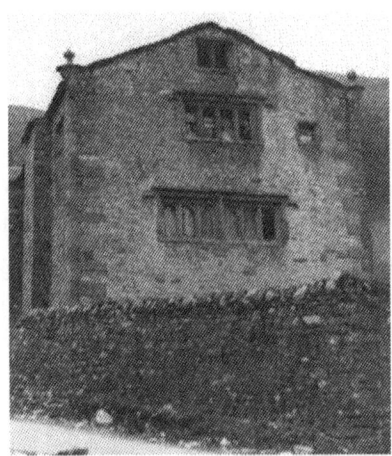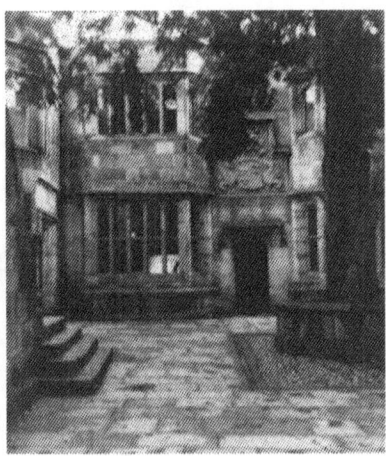

*Left: Mr Cuthbert Wade's house where Lady Anne Clifford stayed on the way
to Skipton Castle.
Right: Conduit Court, Skipton Castle, to which spring water was piped to the castle.
The yew tree was planted in 1659.*

Still following in Lady Anne's footsteps, we searched for her last stopping place before Skipton Castle. This is at Kilnsney, and Mr Cuthbert Wade's house was where she stayed. We found the house to be in a bad state of repair—in fact, it's now a barn. Inside, the first floor is missing, but at wainscot height above where the floor used to be there is a portion of the wall still plastered on which a painted design showed very faintly. How far back this dated I have no idea and, looking round the building, it would take a very strong imagination to visualise what it was like in its heyday.

Skipton Castle, her destination, is in a very different state of repair today than Pendragon, Brougham or Brough. In fact, one can go round today and see the interior which is to a great extent intact. It's interesting to see the kitchen with its great fireplace, its ovens and most interestingly what I took to be the serving hatch. There is a round room, too, where documents were kept—documents that suffered sadly from the ravages of damp and mice.

Cromwell besieged Skipton Castle. It was a heroic resistance, a fact that was acknowledged by the besieging general who, on the eventual surrender, allowed the gallant defenders to march out with honour. The castle was not destroyed, only "sleighted"—that is, the strong top floor which would support cannons was removed and replaced by a lighter one, thus disarming it as a place of resistance. So it remains, with the rest of the building in good repair—thankfully, since it gives us a much better idea of what a castle looked like inside than those ruins which only have a few of their outside walls intact.

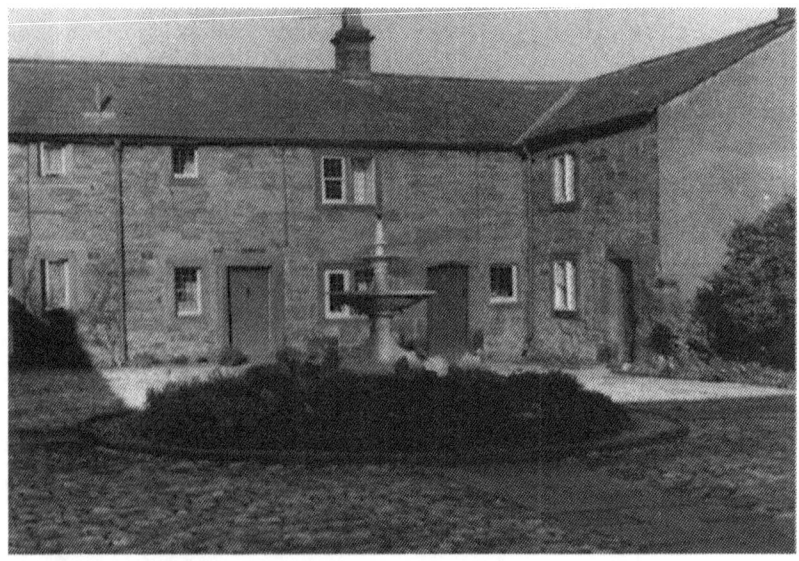

Lady Anne Clifford's almshouses at Appleby.

Lady Anne Clifford was responsible for much building work during her lifetime, but amongst the greatest reminders of her work today are the almshouses at Appleby. Built of local sandstone, they stand just outside the gates of Appleby Castle. They are built in a square around a cobbled courtyard, which is entered through an arched gateway with great doors that are closed and locked every night. What a feeling of security those doors must have given; they are still, no doubt, a comfort to the fortunate tenants today.

When Lady Anne built these almshouses she laid down a set of rules that are adhered to as nearly as possible to this day. The first rule is that these cottages are only for widows living on their own. They may be of any denomination, but another rule says that as long as they are able each must attend a daily service held in the little chapel in a corner of the square. Nowadays the vicar can only conduct a weekly service that they all faithfully attend, the newest member sitting nearest the door—another old custom.

Lady Anne supplied fuel, any coal coming from her own coalmines on Stainmoor and each widow was given a small allowance paid in advance. A very strict rule was applied to this allowance; nothing was to be bought on credit and to do so entailed losing a fortnight's money. Further offences meant expulsion!

A certain day is reserved for scrubbing flags and the spotless flagged and cobbled courtyard bears witness to 300 years of scrubbing! Myra and I entered this courtyard with some trepidation and asked a charming lady at the door of one of the cottages if we could take some photos. She not only gave us permission but offered to show us their little chapel. Light poured through the plain glass window onto the old oak woodwork that shone with the polishing of loving hands over so many years. One could believe that it really was unchanged, especially when one saw the fine brass nailed chest in such wonderful condition; it is the chest that Lady Anne presented to the widows in which to keep their important documents.

When we signed the visitor's book our guide told us how every New Year's Eve they all gather in one of the cottages—including one old lady who needs much help to get there. They sit and sip a glass of sherry while going through the names in the visitor's book, reminiscing about the visitors that visited their chapel the previous year. The evening over, they make sure that the feeble old lady's bed is warm, then take her home and tuck her in. It's a wonderful caring little community and for over 300 years it has functioned so well. Could there be a better tribute to its founder?

31

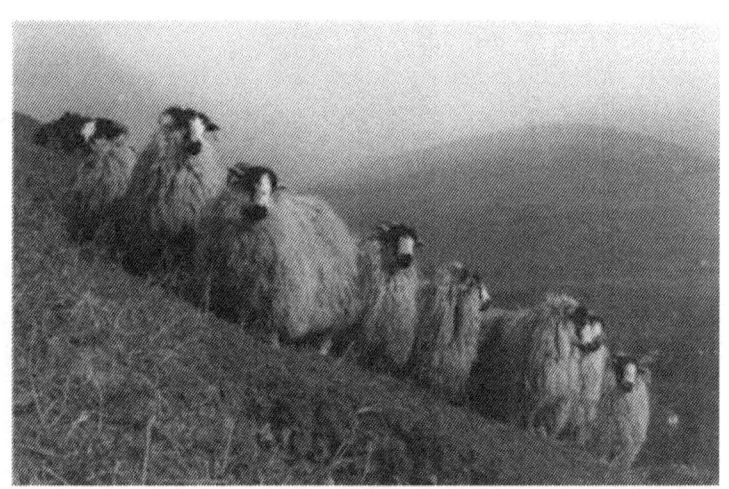

Rough Fell sheep country.

The fells around Sedbergh and Ravenstonedale are the home of the Rough Fell Sheep. Every breed has its enthusiasts but farmers tell me the overriding reason that Roughs are kept here is that it's the breed that thrives best on these fells.

When photographing rams at the Kirkby Stephen ram sales, Myra and I always enjoyed staying with some friends who kept Roughs on a sheep farm that extended three miles over the fells from the village of Ravenstonedale. The farmstead lies in a hollow, the fells sweeping right down to the back door. To reach the farmstead one has to ford a small beck, unless there is a flood when one has to go via the farmyard through a number of gates.

To see Edith's geese and a few hens in the garth anyone would think it was an old-fashioned setting; but make no mistake, the farm—like many hill farms today—is run on modern lines. Using modern methods of stock management, Brian and Edith run this farm with over 700 sheep; and what would the old farmers have said to the sight of a helicopter spreading fertilizer on hillsides too steep for the job to be done with ordinary machinery!

Today with electricity, telephone and a car, life is very different on hill farms; but when winter storms come it's still the same old struggle against the elements for the survival of the flock. Ample supplies must be kept for house and farm because one can be cut off for days or even weeks.

Over the front door are the initials of the man who gave his name to this farm, as well as the date—1684. Lady Anne Clifford had died eight years before the mason carved that date on the lintel but she, in her lifetime, had instigated many building projects among which was the addition of spinning galleries to a number of her properties—probably a very worthwhile proposition in those days, a fact which no doubt others appreciated too. It seems the builder of this place was one of these, for there is a fine example of a spinning gallery under an extended roof at the front of the house.

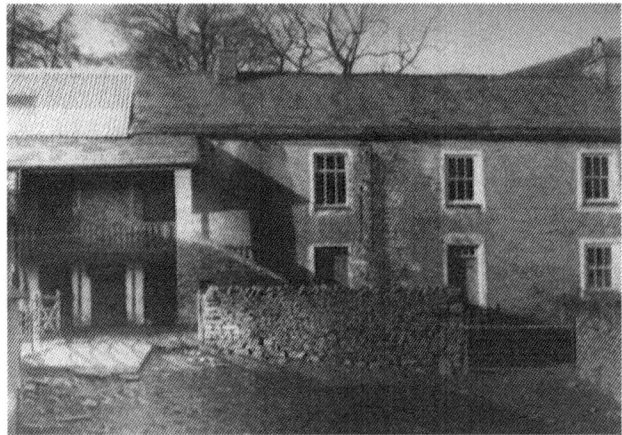

The spinning gallery at Adamthwaite.

The days of home spinning passed, but by the end of the eighteenth century stocking knitting was flourishing round here as it was in other dales at the time. The knitters must have been extremely industrious for it's recorded that the Kendal hosiers used to collect 1000 pairs from the Ravenstonedale district every week, much of the collecting being done with Kendal packhorse teams.

It's uphill whichever way one goes to reach the fell from the house I walked up one day with Brian when he was gathering sheep and noticed the traces of a rough track winding round the shoulder of the fell and I asked if he knew its purpose and where it went. I was told that it was once an alternative route to Sedburgh and, although it was a rough road, was said to have been used in the days of tollgates to avoid paying taxes on the road between Kirkby Stephen and Sedburgh. I wonder if the packhorse teams ever wound their way over this track, either to call at two or three farms on the way to Ravenstonedale to collect stockings or simply to avoid the tollgate. In any case avoiding taxes has been a preoccupation of mankind ever since taxes were invented. This road did make me speculate, however, that there were perhaps other roads in the country that came into being for the same reason.

About the Author

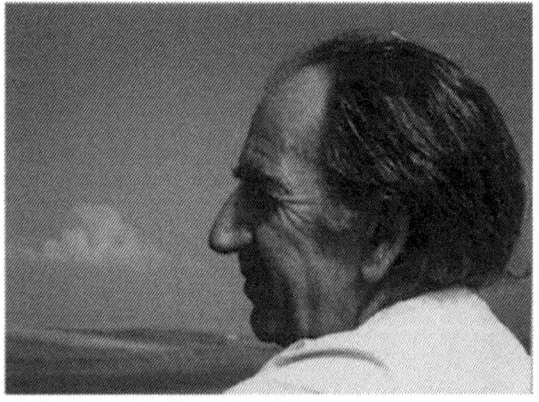

John Moore
Photograph by Myra Moore

Born in a Cumbrian village in 1915, John Moore was involved with farming until he moved into the dales in the '50's. From a child he had always been interested in photography and now took it up as a freelance.

He learnt the art of sheep photography for breeders' flock books and apart from weddings and press work, he became involved in photographic projects in the dales. Meeting so many people in his work, he came to appreciate these sturdy folk of the dales.

www.ingramcontent.com/pod-product-compliance
Lightning Source LLC
Chambersburg PA
CBHW030849180526
45163CB00004B/1512